A JUMBLE OF THOUGHTS TOO

James Sitton

authorHOUSE®

AuthorHouse™
1663 Liberty Drive
Bloomington, IN 47403
www.authorhouse.com
Phone: 833-262-8899

Published by AuthorHouse 06/19/2020

ISBN: 978-1-5462-6290-9 (sc)
ISBN: 978-1-5462-6288-6 (hc)
ISBN: 978-1-5462-6289-3 (e)

Library of Congress Control Number: 2018914396

Print information available on the last page.

This book is printed on acid-free paper.

CONTENTS

In Loving Memory Of My Sister Leslie And My Uncle Mark

For My Three Heartbeats
Maria, Veronica, J.E.S.

"Never lend books; no one ever returns them. The only books I have in my library are books other people have lent me." Anatole France

"Let's start the action!" Frank Sinatra

PREFACE

So it took some time to finally release this book, and it was not for a lack of material. With all that has happened in my life over the past four years I could write a horror novel; a Hallmark Channel Screenplay; a Samuel Daschle Hammett type mystery; an inspired Shakespearian Tragedy, several Dylan Thomas-esc Poems; a Bible Verse Daily Devotional; a *To-Match-Your-Mood Cookbook*; a philosophical self-help book; a joke book; a dirty-joke book; a filthy-joke book; a book on politics (that's the filthy-joke book); a book titled *Romance Finance & Happenstance*. However I was, as matter of duty, morally obliged to write what you are reading now and hopefully about to continue reading.

Isn't it interesting how *Life* has a way of interfering with our lives. These experiences are things my children's grandfather would describe as *things to look forward to looking back on*. Thankfully, time has a way of smoothing out the rougher edges of our memories of life. As more than one friend has mentioned to me over the past few years, *"all that has happened can go in your next book."* Indeed, there are many experiences and many people who have contributed to whom and where I am now. Some people would be happy if I were to write about them; some other people would be scared.. Now that I am retired, I am able to write a *little* more openly than I did in the first book. Not that I wasn't open concerning my opinions previously; but you don't bite the hand that feeds you.

The format of this book is the same as the last; a collection of essays, or another collection of run on sentences. (Punctuation like fornication is more fun with no rules.) Once again, the purpose of this book is to make you think. Also, hope it brings some joy and amusement to your day. Again, there are opinions within to offend just about everyone, so there is no need to feel special. Even if you do not care for me personally, (opinions about me do vary), you will still be able to enjoy at least some parts of this book, it is that good. Then again…

Something you will not often read in a non-fiction book is for the author to ask the reader to research everything within said book; yet this is exactly what I am asking you to do. If I have made a mistake or am flat out wrong, please let me know. If that indeed it turns out to be the case, I will make certain to correct it in future editions or in subsequent books. My goal with these books, other than to be financial pleasure, is to entertain, impart knowledge and most important, to make you think.

There is a difference between stating a fact and stating an opinion and I have tried to make it very clear when I am writing one or the other. Challenge me, I challenge you. Knowledge may not be power, but you must have knowledge of what to do with your power or you will lose it. Moving on.

As before, just because something is in print doesn't make it right; but it does give you, the reader, the experience of agreeing or disagreeing with what is written. Hopefully not everyone will agree with all of my opinions; that would be boring. Hopefully you will find some of these subjects interesting. I look forward to hearing from you…unless you are offended; in which case there is no need to complain, I am sorry already.

Cheers,
James
e-mail: james.sitton@hotmail.com.
For Speaking/Question & Answer Event Requests Contact : ajotjs@gmail.com

BOOKS

"If a book be false in its facts, disprove them; if false in
its reasoning, refute it. But for God's sake, let us freely
hear both sides if we choose." Thomas Jefferson

With so many books procurable from the twisted minds of so many self-absorbed people, how could anyone decide upon something to read and why would someone choose my book before any other book which had been written before? It took a minute, but I settled upon an answer, *vanity*. That was the basic marketing strategy of the first book. Everyone has it and it just so turns out I may be loaded with it. Why else would I bother to stay in shape at forty-seven with three children.

Choosing something to read is not something most of people my age or younger have a lot of experience with. For most of our lives we have not needed to make that choice. Our parents gave us Dr. Seuss. Our teachers gave us reading lists. Our churches gave us verses. Our jobs gave us manuals. Our romantic interludes gave us letters. Our heartaches gave us poems and songs. Our Aunts gave us the Bible and our Uncles gave us Playboy.

As time passed recreational reading became a luxury in which we could indulge, but it had to compete with our twenty-something/thirty-something lives. We stopped working at a job and began establishing a career. Recreational reading often took a backseat to dating, drive-thru-meals, *choir practice, girlfriends-to fiancé-to matrimony. Then came *What To Expect When You Are Expecting* (yes ladies, men read it too.) By the way, Dr. Spock has absolutely nothing to do with *Star Trek*; in fact he never even mentions it. Before you know it, you are right back to reading Dr. Seuss, to your children.

So why read this book? Well, (that's a deep subject.), it truly is a book for everybody and anybody: You may burn it if you are a pyromaniac. You may read it more than once if you have a multi-personality disorder. Go ahead and steal it if you are a kleptomaniac, preferably from a friend rather than a store; (Encouraging illegal activity is not something I want to do...also I would like to receive some royalties.) If you are a sadist, you can always read it aloud to somebody else. There is something contained herein to irate and aggravate just about everyone...give it time. Obviously I do not mind someone being offended by, or disagreeing with something I say or write; at least it shows they were paying attention.

Enjoy

*In the U.S. Border Patrol if you and your fellow agents decided to have a beer or three after the shift was over it was not called Happy Hour; It was called *Choir Practice*. ("Sorry sweetheart, no can do; I have *choir practice* after work today.")

THE ARCH OF LIFE

"Never look back unless you are planning to go
that way." -Henry David Thoreau

For a couple of years in the 1980s, I attended junior high school in a suburb of St. Louis, Missouri. Not a mere middle school, like my younger siblings would go to, but a proper junior high school, Crestview Jr. High School (CJHS). Moving from Florida and leaving the structure of St, Bernadette Catholic School behind, I attended CJHS for the seventh and eighth grade. Those years would prove to be significant in my adolescent journey from child to teenager. Athletics, electives, puberty, peer groups, the cheerleaders, were all contained and on display within a two story, (and basement), public school building and its surrounding campus.

"I don't know what I've got; but I am about to share it!" Bob Hope

Outside the teenage social hierarchy of CJHS stood the Arch of St. Louis; the Gateway Arch; Gateway to the West. Completely oblivious to the symbolism I would attribute to this structure later in my life, the simplistic beauty and strength of the Arch was not lost on my fourteen year old self. (Building blocks and Legos helped my understanding of the strength of an arch well before Geometry.) My mid-forty year old self no longer thinks of the St. Louis Arch as "the Gateway to the West"; for me, it is not a gateway to a physical frontier but a philosophical one. Not a path to a place or state but a pathway to a state of being. The physical structure an arch is how one would traditionally structure a story. The *hero's journey* as defined and described by Joseph Campbell follows this pattern. A person's life story can be represented by an arch. (Does this mean I am referring to me or anyone else as a hero? No; but if this is your life story, go ahead; we all want to be the star of our own movie.)

If you stand at the base of the Arch in St. Louis at mid-day and look up, you can follow the ascending lines of brilliant silver reflecting in the sun. It looks like a path to follow, leading to something more or to heaven. We all follow a path, a way to gaining, knowledge, control, confidence, and leadership. Along my path, or life, I rarely questioned how high is too high or how far was too far. You make life your own by defining how you choose to live it. We exist in the state of self and as we grow so does our sense of self alongside our personal desires. It is our natural state of being. Allow me the liberty to speak for us all; we crave love, food, knowledge, comfort, faith (in something), sex, money, power, prestige, acceptance, happiness, and forgiveness.

Despite life itself and myself sometimes getting in the way of my life, I consider this life I choose to live a blessed one. There was a period of time I wanted for nothing. It was as if I had finally found that perfect uplifting song to add to the otherwise melancholy soundtrack of my life. The very reason I may still be alive is due to the debt I owe God considering I have been living on credit from Him; some may refer to this as Grace. Not simply surviving, but actually living. Never did I feel the need to create a *bucket list* because my entire life has been one extraordinary experience after another; be those experiences good or bad. For a time I felt as though I had reached the zenith of my life. There were achievements at work, achievements at home and I had what I thought to be a general understanding of this world. However, except from vending machines, change is inevitable.

Back to Joseph Campbell and all the stories, myths, and legends from various cultures throughout history. After the protagonist in a story preservers or survives the unimaginable and reaches what at the time seems to be the pinnacle of life, or the story, something happens and then the fall happens. This is what makes these stories compelling and relatable. Most of us fall down. It is at this point anyone could lose focus. With lost focus and unstable balance, you may easily find yourself falling towards disaster. It is a scary thing to realize there are greater things to fear in life than death. When we fall, we stop looking towards the heavens, or to heaven with hope or for hope. It is easy to allow our heads to hang and just stare at the dirt. Pain is what is remembered from past experiences. Yet time seems to have a way of smoothing out the rougher edges of pain. When we are at our lowest, we seem to sink lower, or at least I do. (If I heard anyone speak to a child in the same manner I speak to myself in those moments, God have mercy on them.)

When I was at what I believed to be my lowest it seemed all was lost and

I thought there was no more for me. Well, I've been mistaken before, and I'm certain I'll be wrong again. It may be easy to wallow within the tragedies which seem to dominate and shape our lives. It is understandable how we may tend to focus on those painful moments that knocked us down. But we must stand back up and remember we have Grace from God on our side. I was shown or you may say received mercy. When that happens, when you notice your own tears, it allows you to see the tears on those people around you. Too late, you realize how much has been lost, but you thank God that you are able to recognize how much more there is to lose. Ultimately you understand we live not only for desire but for hope and to give hope.

When I realized how in many ways my self-determination may have actually betrayed my actual desires, I was retired, single and in another airport. No one would be waiting for me at my destination that day. There were no appointments and no engagements for me to keep. There was no one to offer an apology and there was no one present for me to forgive. After you take your time introducing rock to bottom there is an opportunity, if you take it, a moment; you may notice you recall more than the difficult, more than the agony. You are able to focus on the pleasant and the beautiful. I did and when I did, I wanted it again! At that moment you can look back on your life up to where you are; you can look back upon the Arch of your life. You may even be looking back and up...perhaps up towards heaven. We all have decisions to make throughout our lives. To simply continue on the path I had found myself on was not what I wanted. Walking back up to the Arch and beginning another journey is what I wanted.. If you fall, you are not dead. Your troubles, failures, heartbreak and pain did not and cannot eat you. Realizing there was no fat lady singing and I had yet to light my last cigar, my story, the story is not over. Your story is not over. Previous experiences, good and bad are assets not baggage. You don't have to check them. They do not have to slow you down or hold you back.

All of a sudden you may once again notice things around you and realize you cannot notice everything. The blessing you have and the opportunities you have yet to identify are all there. Hope returns followed by desire. Positive memories overshadow hurt. You remember we are the sum of what we achieve not what we intend. Then one day I noticed a vivacious red head lady smiling... it was then perhaps, I realized the zenith of my life had yet to be reached.

That's Enough

FREE SPEECH

Everything you say will be misquoted and used against your grandchildren.

This topic has been in the national debate lately and as the Presidential election cycle approaches, wait, too late, it is already here, (Like merchants pushing Christmas season, it keeps starting earlier.), the conversation will only increase or the noise will just get louder. No one likes to be told they are wrong. Being told you are wrong is especially unpopular when it is true. So this essay should be pretty unpopular among the masses. (Which you, the reader of this essay, are not. You, yes I am writing *you* specifically. You are an exceptional person with terrific taste [in literature] and an inquisitive mind possessing stunning intellect. Otherwise *you* would not be reading this book; otherwise *you* would be one of *them*.) By the way, later in this book I have an essay concerning labels and why they are ridiculous which *we* already know...

Okay, back on point now. With regards to the First Amendment, it has four distinct parts. This essay will only focus on one of them. So, before discounting my points, I simply ask that you read all of them first; afterwards, by all means, open season, fire away! I welcome every dispute and/or counterpoint from the sharpshooters out there. Seriously, debate makes life interesting; Elevated voice volumes and high octave levels do not. I have an octave filter with a centre frequency of 1kHz, so anything above an upper frequency of 1.414kHz, (aka default level of an ex-lover's voice...). Therefore, I will not be yelled at, nor will I yell at you. Agreed? Good; now let's fight as God intended, civilized.

Most of what citizens think they know about the freedom of speech is incorrect if not flat out wrong. Without education, their arguments and debates come across as guileful and only create noise. (You see, no one is listening, [I love that expression...to *see* who is not *listening*...it just strikes me as funny.], which is probably fine since no one seems to know what they are talking about.) Before you go *Cool Hand Luke on me, keep patient and keep reading. Hopefully this essay will clear the air; drown out the noise insert cliché; add one more; now end the sentence.

Our Constitution states:

Amendment 1: Congress shall make no law respecting an establishment of religion, or prohibiting the free exercise thereof; or abridging the freedom of speech, or of the press; or the right of the people peaceably to assemble, and to petition the Government for a redress of grievances.

Okay, as mentioned before, the Amendment has four parts; to make it simple they are: 1. Laws about religion. 2. Freedom to worship/practice religion. 3. Freedom of speech against the federal government and the government's policies. 4. The right to petition the federal government.

Just for attestation, let us skip the first eighteen words and the last twenty-three words of the amendment and focus on (the flip side of As Tears Go By) only four words; *the freedom of speech.* The other topics mentioned: religion, the press, assembly and redress of grievances, are issues for other essays at another time.

So what does the amendment say and what right(s) does it give us with regards to speaking? I will explain the concept in four ways using both positive and negative facts to make the points:

1. In the context written, the freedom of speech means the federal government cannot stop you from speaking against or about itself, the federal government. The man cannot stop you from complaining about the man.
2. The freedom prevents the U.S. Government from punishing people for expressing their opinions and concerns about the government.
3. It does not protect people from repercussions at work or in public from voicing their opinions.
4. It does not give you right to say, whatever you want to say, to whomever you want to say it to, wherever you want to say it.

This is very important; please teach your children this; tell your friends; spread the word. Being exegesis is important with regards to this issue. *You can be fired from your job for something you say or do and it is not illegal for an employer to do so.* Company policy will stand a legal test.

You may be sued by a private citizen for defamation of character or slander.

- You may be charged with disturbing the peace.
- You may be indicted for inciting a riot.
- Okay, fine, I'll say it, "It" fine, you may be fined.

Okay, for the sake of argument; you are correct in stating anyone may say anything they want whenever they want to whomever they want at any time they want. I'll give you that if you will recognize for the sake of augury, anyone doing so must face and accept the consequences for it. Because this is not a constitutionally protected right. Agreed? What, no? Okay, let me continue.

When these discussions reach the high court, the specifics surrounding the issue are not the issue. The law, as written, is the issue. Circumstantial evidence has nothing to do with Constitutional Law. If circumstances surrounding events and details concerning actions have an impact upon the Constitutionality of or our rights and how they are enforced or applied, then we have NO Rights Guaranteed Under The Constitution as stipulated. It would mean our Constitutional Rights are not guaranteed, but subject to opinion based upon circumstances and events. If your *Rights* are subject to what another person thinks about what you did, you have *no rights.*

The law would not be binding and our rights would not be guaranteed.

That means no justice and no liberty. That is not a right but a gift.

There is a danger in that because anything given can be taken away. This should lead to caution about legislating from the bench; something not supposed happen yet it does. If you disagree, I'm going to need you to get way off my back on this for now. We can debate it later.

It is important when discussing and debating rights and liberty to stick to the issue and the Constitution as written. Emotion, sympathy and empathy have no place when determining the constitutionality of _____.

There is some confusion about this wonderful right of ours, *the freedom of speech,* circulating about at the moment. This latest national discussion concerning the 1st Amendment is the result of actions taken by athletes and comments concerning those actions taken by athletes, made by government representatives. How deep is this discussion? Well, (that's a deep subject), the debate over if the athlete had the right to make a gesture as a statement has superseded the statement the athlete claimed he was trying to make.

Clear as a glass of muddy water. But it shouldn't be; it is very simple.

Employees do not have a Constitutional right to free speech or freedom of expression at work. So employers, all employers, are generally free to restrict employee speech, at least while they are at work being paid.

Amendment 1 of the U.S. Constitution is not as broad as many people think it is. Don't misunderstand me or think I am making light of this right or the importance of it, because I am not and it is important. Consider the point in history when this right was written. Important and significant are words which really fail describe, well the importance or significance of the Amendment.

In today's Face-opinion-Book-post-a-complaint-a-Tweet-a-Insta-bitch-a-gram society of ours, it may be difficult to understand how unique the ability to publically disagree with one's government still is. Understand this, countries proclaiming their citizens have the right or even the ability to call their government to account without repercussions are not in the majority.

Okay back to the recent incident(s) igniting the freedom of speech debate. Please allow my brief five sentence summary. 1. A NFL Quarterback knelt during the National Anthem before the start of a ballgame to bring attention to Civil Liberties/Rights, specifically groups of minorities facing discrimination. 2. The NFL states kneeling during the National Anthem is a violation of League Policy. 3. The President declares the action disrespectful, suggests boycotting NFL. 4. Other NFL players kneel in support of their colleague. 5. Emotions escalate, everyone has an opinion, and no one cites the law or our actual rights.

Would everyone agree that is a very basic summary? (Of course not, but let me continue so everyone will be offended.) The civil rights statement is not the issue being discussed and the reason is ego and everyone involved is at fault. Yes, good old fashion ego/vanity/self-righteous-holier-than-thou behavior. After the QB's action/statement and the League's policy statement, every news conference's questions and answers were not about the state of Civil Rights and Liberties but about the QB's right to make a statement/any statement vs the Leagues right to stop him. A simple "I knelt to bring attention to the daily struggle minorities face with regards to their civil rights and liberties." statement could have followed, it didn't. The NFL said not while working. The QB could have held a press conference after the fact to bring attention to discrimination, inequality and whatever else he wanted. That did not happen. Had the other NFL players made a statement agreeing with the QB's position with regards to Civil Rights/Liberties, it would have kept the issue of minorities and civil rights in the spotlight. Instead, the statement was *we support our fellow colleague's right to make a statement.* This made the issue about them and about the QB, not about the little guy or minorities. A simple statement from the NFL stating "we are not the government, this is a company, this is our policy" may have still kept the issue about Civil Rights/Liberties/Minorities the issue; we'll never know. Finally, why did the government make a statement? The action didn't legally involve the government. Do you see how the issue got lost in the sea of egos? The people involved became the issue rather than the people the QB said were facing discrimination. That is vanity. I know vanity, I'm loaded with it.

An employer cannot make you say something, but they can prevent you from saying anything if you want to keep your job. Generally speaking, if any employer gave you notice about company policy prohibited actions, you cannot say, "Screw you, I'm saying it anyway." and expect to keep your job. It is not a right; you are not protected and it is not a federal issue.

The real problem with this situation is, the QB did have an important social issue to discuss. But no one is discussing the social issue. They are discussing whether a highly paid athlete was treated unfairly by an entertainment company; so much for bringing attention to social issues in an attempt to bring about change or improvement through active dialog and intelligent debate. Nope. Now, instead of looking into police shootings and claims of excessive use of force everyone is talking about whether a quarterback was let go due to race. That is the issue now, so much for priorities...congratulations to everyone involved. You have now exceeded my ability to give a damn. What a bang-up-job everybody! Screw inner-city kids, or whomever, a quarterback lost his million-dollar contract. Pathetic. (I can see a book review now quoting me out of context, *James Sitton says screw inner-city children.*)

A private place of business or website or school does not have to put up with you. Guess what? Neither do the rest of us. But congratulations on your Nike endorsement deal. You all knew about that right? The QB got fat endorsement deal from Nike. Yeah, Nike doubled down and has chosen to use race relations to sell shoes. Classy.

Set, Hike!

*(run off...get "rabbit in your blood")

THE MURDERING MONSTER OF MY SISTER

The police investigation concerning the death of my sister is still open. While I do not want to jeopardize the investigation or taint the opinion of a potential jury, I have decided to light a fire here to get some movement.

My years of training and of training criminal investigators and special agents of the Federal Government has provided me with the skills and background to conduct an investigation of my own into the death of my sister. Everything discovered, all evidence and reports of my findings have been given to the investigative authorities. My investigation into the death of my sister Leslie has led me to certain conclusions.

While I am not going to list everything here, I will state, based upon my years of experience, my sister, in my professional opinion, was murdered by her husband. Perhaps I probably should not come right out and say David Lovelace is a murderer; I can say based upon my own investigation and professional experience, I believe David Lovelace is a murderer and responsible for the death of my sister Leslie.

As I mentioned before, I have purposely left out information. The case is still open. David even attempted to retrieve his gun used in the incident but could not as it is still considered evidence.

My parents asked me to give the eulogy at Leslie's funeral, which was the most difficult speech I have ever delivered. After the funeral, we all went to the home of my cousin and her family. The husband of my little sister, Leslie, the lady we had just buried, started completing the life-insurance policy claim forms at the kitchen counter of my cousin's home. It was sickening. Now I understand that previous statement is subjective and not objective.as there is no way for me to prove his filling out an insurance claim form was sickening. So let me change that statement to, "the sight of his action made me feel sick." There, I am legally covered in case the bastard wants to sue me.

11

Once he is locked up, my sister's children will be taken care of. Her two boys may live with my family, or my other sister and her family, or with my brother, or with my parents or even with my cousin's family. The boys will be fine once that monster is locked away. Oh, yes, locked up, for life. You don't send evil into hell; that would be like tossing Brer Rabbit into the briar patch. No death sentence but life in prison. I'll personally pay the medical bills to keep that son-of-a-bitch alive in a cell and start a foundation to keeps the funds going towards them after I'm gone.

Turn Around David, Times Up

LANGUAGE

"Watch your language." Said By Every Parent At Some Point
"To say nothing, especially when speaking, is half
the art of diplomacy" Will Durant

In case you have not noticed by this series of books, I love language; punctuation not so much. Using language is something I simply enjoy, and I love confusing people with it. When I was a boy and was told to watch my language, I responded with something about agreeing to keep a closer eye on my books…or something…It didn't go well.

Using language to say what I mean and not what people may think I mean is fun. Not using certain words so my true intent or meaning will be understood only by those whom are paying attention and hopefully not until I have *gone Elvis* aka, left the building, I find to be particularly enjoyable.

The Gospel according to John: In the beginning was the Word, and the Word was with God and the Word was God.

Linguist Ferdinand Saussure wrote he *saw a thing and its name as having a totally arbitrary relationship and we really do not know things; but only access their shadows through language in which everything has a meaning in the context of a system we have created.*

Aren't language and life are connected? The expression of thoughts, the descriptions of events, even something as basic of the names of things and people. A car is a car. Frank Sinatra is Frank Sinatra. Then again, perhaps it is what it is because we say it is so…

That's, That's What I Think

PROLIFERATION

At some point early in this century I left the world of smuggling people and dope and entered the world of, um, smuggling items. As my friend and my former training officer, Bob "Buck" Most, told me over lunch shortly before I left Texas for another agency, "Smuggling is smuggling and sign-cutting is the same no matter where you are or what you are looking for; something is always is left behind and something is always taken away; just look for it." He was right and it was a perfect bookend to what he told me the first time I worked with him.

We, (Well not really *we,* it was him.), were tracking a group of illegals heading North through the brush in South Texas about twenty-some-odd miles from Laredo, TX. Being a trainee on my first swing shift, I was as useless as a husband in the delivery room; only there for company. At one point we lost the *sign, and would lose the group if we couldn't pick it up again. Using a semi-circle pattern from the point we lost the tracks, we searched for any indication of their direction. Since we were so far behind the group there was no danger they might hear us. (Usually you would be a quiet as possible.) So, my training officer Buck took the opportunity to explain the following; "People are like water and will take the easiest route. So when you lose the sign, or just plain lost, "look up from the ground and look around you and ask yourself *which way would you go?*"

Proliferation was a word I had never used in a sentence much less thought about before I left the areas of Texas and Mexico I eventually grew to love. There was no way of knowing how much my life would revolve around that simple word.

In 2001 we as a country faced a new enemy which was not fully understood and still isn't understood in my opinion. The U.S.A. was also dealing with four hostile nations, (most will tell you there were three at that time, I disagree.). Added to this nonsense, the U.S.A. also had the usual suspects of adversarial and passive-aggressive nations behaving as a younger sibling possessing picture of you drag-racing your father's car and waiving it around in an attempt to intimidate you.

Denying weapons or disrupting the procurement networks of certain nations, groups, even individuals became my mission and part of the greater U.S.A. strategy. Nuclear-Proliferation, Chemical-Biological Weapons, WMD, are all words which became part of our national discussion and my daily world. We and our allies learned how our borders were being exploited and how antiquated export control regulations were and still are. Our efforts and objectives to counter proliferation of deemed exports must be updated. The targets of our advisories have changed as fast as new technologies are developed and the world seems to still have an issue understanding Universities and research institutions are part of the new battlefields.

Export Control Regulations, Licensing Requirements, Arms Export Control Act, The Proliferation Security Initiative and every other measure of *Alphabet Soup* used to combat illicit transshipment of military and dual use technologies are valuable and necessary components of an overall strategy but the fact is they are not enough and not keeping pace with changing adversaries and new technologies. Quite frankly, it is frightening. We now find ourselves in a state of perpetual war. Good for the military industrial complex, bad in every other way. The Cold War was essentially an *armed truce* based upon the understanding of mutual annihilation and obliteration of the planet. The Cold War was comfortable in that each side clearly knew who their enemy was, what they possessed, and what was necessary to counter. Compared to what we face in today's world, this actually seems like a reasonable compromise between the U.S.A. and FSU. That's crazy!

Nuclear weapons under the control of Pakistan, DPRK, and what the hell, just go ahead and add Iran to the list, makes the availability of these weapons and systems to terrorist organizations, hostile nations, and even individuals more prevalent than ever. An economic depressed DPRK manufacturing nuclear weapons is scary. The idea of them selling those weapons to a rouge actor/nation, would be all of the worst parts of the Bible. With one sale, DPRK can solve two major problems; their revenue stream and a delivery system for their weapons. Why bother with an intercontinental missile delivery system when you can sell a weapon in a backpack and maybe even suggest where it should be deployed?

When it comes to how to deter proliferation of sophisticated weapons from reaching small actors unconstrained by alliances, nothing is certain. This is no longer a bi-polar Cold War era world. Always do we appear to be surprised by events and seem to lack the understanding of cultural barriers to objective strategy. The world is stuck, we lost the sign. It is time to look up, look around us, and ask which way would you go; because the unpopular but truth is this; proliferation is an issue that is more dangerous now than it was when I first used the word in a sentence.

Pray

DON'T BOTHER CALLING, I'M SORRY ALREADY

Letters are such a joy. There are not many things that are capable of transporting you back in time to a feeling…except maybe music or pictures… or home movies…or movies…or the aroma of certain food…or electronic correspondence. Okay, alright, I take it back; many things can take you back. But at a cost of forty some-odd cents per letter I think letters are the best value. (Correspondence, don't be an ass; you know full well I was not referring to specific letters of the alphabet costing forty cents each. [Oh, I meant ass in the Biblical sense; i.e. our Lord rode into the city on an ass.] Don't be a beast of burden.) Moving on.

With all of the times I have relocated as both a child and as an adult, it is surprising I have been able to keep anything of mine much less the letters I have received over the years. But I have…boxes of them. The federal government was nice enough to hold them in storage for me for most of my career. There are boxes that I had not opened in twenty years. It was not until I retired that I had the time to actually go through some of these great pieces of nostalgia. Let me tell you about one of them.

Without meaning to sound as if I am bragging, I have a terrific memory. It is both a blessing and a curse. This made me very good at my job and allowed me to write excellent after action reports. The problem with a good memory is it doesn't allow you to filter out anything unpleasant; you remember all of it.

A clear conscience is usually the sign of a selective memory.

The good, the bad, and the ugly, (insert classic spaghetti western echoing whistle here), that is life and you learn to take the good with the bad. What choice do you have? Let us skip the bad for a moment and focus on something positive, something good, and something pure. Do you remember your first crush? The first time you got that awesome yet scary feeling of realizing you like someone in a romantic way? Well, maybe not romance. I was in the fourth grade when I developed a crush on a girl in my class. At that age I couldn't define romance, but I knew something was different. She sat in front of me and her name was Lisa.

As I mentioned, it wasn't until recently that I found and went through a box of old letters. It was amazing; contained within were letters going back to 1984. Like many of you, I was forced to move around a lot in childhood. Not because my parents were active duty military with required relocation which many of you may be familiar with. Not because my father was broad minded and had to stay one step ahead of the sheriff. Nope, you see I am a child of divorce and it wasn't until high school I actually stayed in the same school for any length of time. Lisa sat in front of me when I attended Most Holy Redeemer MHR in Tampa Florida. At the time my sister and I were suitcase kids alternating between two households. This was not something I ever considered to be a negative thing, it was just how it was.

I was pretty fortunate in that my parents and step parents never teased me about having a crush. In fact, when I wanted to write Lisa a poem, I remember asking for help. This particular week, I was with my father and step-mother. While still at the dinner table after dinner, I asked them for help. It was my desire to write the *Rose Are Red* poem, but didn't know how to spell *violets*, so I asked for help. My step-mother, being a school teacher, told me something that she stills tells me to this day, "*Look it up.*" (As mentioned in the last book, I have had the same dictionary throughout most of my career and at some point I began to underline every word I looked up. It is amazing how many times I have looked up the same word. What does that have to do with this essay? Absolutely nothing.)

Anyway, I gave Lisa the poem and for a brief period of time we would hang out during recess. I say a brief period of time because for several months that school year, I wasn't allowed to go to recess. Not because of behavioral problems; because I was lazy and didn't want to memorize my multiplication tables. I was the only one in the class that failed a test and my teacher made me stay in the classroom to study those darn multiplication tables until I was able to complete one-hundred problems in one minute. The kicker was, I had to take that test in front of the entire class. I never thanked that teacher, so I am doing it now. I am so very blessed to have had people that really cared and care about me. Unfortunately I am not certain a teacher, any teacher, these days would be permitted to do something such has hold a child back from recess. From what I can see, many parents would complain that their precious offspring was being singled out and make some sort of complaint to the school. That is too bad. When I was growing up every adult was not only allowed to *parent* any child, it was expected. Does anyone else remember those days? The days when you couldn't get away with anything? If I was running from my parents I wouldn't get far because some random adult was likely to stick their leg out and trip me, ending my escape…and my parents would have thanked them for it. Now I that I am a parent, I am not going to comment on anyone else's parenting style (yes I am) because I realize that parenting is a difficult thankless job (no it isn't…thankless) and there is no guide book (that is correct, there is not one, there are many) out there to help you navigate your child through the stages of childhood. (You don't need one, you were a child; if you don't like the way you were raised, do the opposite with your children.) I do have question for those of you insulted by the statements I just made. If you are truly doing such a bang-up job as a parent, why is your twenty-five year old son still living at home? (This does not apply to Mexican or Puerto Rican men. I understand the culture and honestly if my mother treated me like a prince, cooked for me at all hours, did my laundry, gave me money she took from my father and basically let me get away with anything and helped me do it, I would be living at home and taking dates to hotels claiming the *traveling card* as well. By the way, this is not an insult; I am impressed! How do you do that?)

Where was I before judging other parents but not being insensitive to other cultures…ah yes, going through a box of old letters. Now if I told you that I have kept just about every letter I have ever received you may think I was exaggerating. Well, (deep subject), guess what I found recently? I found a letter from Lisa. Yes, the Lisa from fourth and fifth grade. Why would I bring up a letter from some random Lisa written two years ago? "Hold it! Hold it!" Lisa from two years ago, I appreciate your letter and have kept it. Thank you. Anyway, MHR Lisa and I had written each other letters after I moved from Tampa to Round Rock Texas and I found one. Yep…how cool is that? You can't hold an e-mail or a text. Well, you can; but printing it is not the same. There is something special about actually holding something that someone created for you. To hold what they held is much more personal than simply re-reading something someone wrote. Or perhaps I am too sentimental.

Just as in my previous book, if you disagree with anything I have written or if I have made a mistake, let me know; my e-mail address is in the Preface.

Feel free to contact for positive reasons as well…and if I have really offended you, in the words of Craig Ferguson, *I look forward to your letters.* (E-mail me for a physical address.)

That's Enough

Have You Ever Considered

STAYING ALIVE

**by the BeeGees
is the perfect tempo to administer CPR?**

ENEMY ADVISORY

Why did kamikaze pilots wear helmets?

Different societies view problems and objectives in different ways. Attempting to understand these differences is vital to all aspects of foreign policy. Social characteristics and social conditioning are deeply rooted in every society and this influences how the world is viewed. No subject in the world is more complex than foreign affairs, except maybe divorce and family court.

Life's A Beach v Take That Beach!

If your objective is to take a beach, how would you do it? Blitz (blitzkrieg – it may be of new information to some, but the now popular football term is actually a German for *1. lighting 2. military strategy-an intensive or sudden military attack by combined forces.*) This was the most popular way in the past. Not so long ago, if the Russians wanted to take a to take a beach, superior forces sent all at once would simply over run the area and claim the beach. But then the Chinese perfected a more subtle way which is just as effective, must lest costly in both gold and treasure, (money and lives), and often before their target has any idea of what's occurring before it's too late.

If the Chinese want to take a beach, they send a few people at a time to the beach to grad a hand full of sand, put in in their pocket and walk away. It may take a minute, but you do not need to build a tank. You do not need to train and fund army. Most important, you don't receive any attention from the rest of the world until your objective is all but successful. The Chinese didn't invent the method any more than the Allies storming the beaches of Normandy or Russia, basically invading everywhere; most recently the

Ukraine all in the name of *Novorossiya*. But they certainly have it mastered. Who is to say which method is best as long as you obtain your objective?

For anyone who studies intelligence and military strategy, the French *Farewell Dossier* is pretty much required reading. During the 80s, before the FSU collapsed, (*Former Soviet Union,* not the college in Florida), a *KGB operative was flipped by French Intelligence. Through their asset, the French learned of a network of Soviet agents activities concerning the proliferation of western technologies. Proliferation, reverse engineering, and having agents working for and studying in foreign companies and universities are all reasons the FSU was able to stay competitive with their adversaries. These activities prompted the U.S.A. and her allies to establish export control laws. Many of these regulations were the basis for United Nations sanctions in the 1990s, 2000s, 2010s. These sanctions were possible in part due to actions by Ronald Reagan who signed legislation creating an agency to enforce export control laws, and combat, investigate, infiltrate and disrupt the activities of those involved. Long before the September 11, 2001 terrorists attacks on the U.S.A. and the Patriot Act, several department agencies with different authorities were working together in basically what we now call Joint Task Forces. If you never heard about this the reason is simple, you don't let your enemy know what actions you are taking against them. It was not until 2012 activities really began to hit the press, which informed the public but damaged a nation and endangered the world. So either good or bad or catastrophic, depending on what you believe in. (Oh, I am not referring to Edward Snowden nor Chelsea Manning.)

Back to the *Farewell Dossier;* in the 80's when the French intelligence was shared with the U.S.A. a strategic decision was made. Opinions varied, as they often do. Both sides of the issue make logical sense. Unfortunately that is the way the world works. With the intelligence, the world stage once again found a way to become more dangerous.

There are always two sides to consider when making a decision and there are always three sides to a conflict. With a conflict, the sides are easily identifiable; as long as you yourself are not engaged in the conflict. There is the view of aggrieved party *A*. There is the view of aggrieved party *B*. Then there is the truth, which is usually, but not always, somewhere in-between. Our versions of events, truth and our reality are often a result of our personal perspective and positions. Where we stand on an issue often depends upon where we sit. By the time the French intelligence reached her allies, a clear decision had to be made. It was a choice between destroying a network which had empowered an aggressive enemy and would continue to do so, or to let the network continue, monitor the activities, and respond accordingly. The classic, devil you know versus the one you don't. Personally, I do not subscribe to the "lessor of two evils" description of choices. No such thing exists, evil is evil, you just decide upon your course of action.

> Both Choices will hurt you,
> No choice will destroy you.

Historian Samuel Huntington wrote the end of the Cold War may re-ignite "*a clash of civilizations*" and warned "*ethnic, religious, and nationalist passions would return.*" Serbia's ethnic cleansing of Bosnia...the Hutu genocide... Tutsis in Rwanda...tribalism in Sudan, Syria, and Somalia...ISIS...Turkey and the Kurds...could all be viewed as examples. *Unlike the Cold War which was a political and ideological conflict, these examples are about race, religion, territory, and nationalism.*

With regards to Islamic Terrorists or Extremists we will never completely understand our enemy's mind, luckily they do not understand ours either. But you must attempt to understand an adversary's motives because once actions begin, you find yourself in the closest of all relationships, war. Like or not, in war, you will be close with your enemies for quite some time. (Kinda like going through a divorce.) This is what makes good intelligence so important. It is helpful to identify who your enemies really are, discover what they want, and try to understand what they believe in. I'm not suggesting without those three basic pieces of information you won't win, but without that knowledge, you are certainly going to bleed, a lot. The U.S.A. is and has been bleeding a lot. We find ourselves engaged with people many do not understand.

This enemy combatant maintains fanatical beliefs in what they view as *God's will* and their destiny to control the planet. To this end, treachery, brutality, rape and torture are all justified if used against any non-Muslims, the infidels. With no resemblance of western values, they can inflict damage on enemies of superior number with superior weapons. They have no regard for civilians or collateral damage. They have no respect for life, even their own. They have no government, represent no country. Their prophet is their spiritual leader and their political ruler which is a dangerous combination of the supernatural and the terrestrial. Religion and politics intertwined into blind allegiance. Imagine a leadership with the executive authority of the President, a Prime Minister, then add the spiritual authority of the Pope, the Archbishop of Canterbury, the head of the Orthodox Church, and then, add blessings of God, then you may begin to understand what jihad means to them. Like Hirohito meant to the Japanese, Mohamad is everything to Islam. Like Shintoism, Islam is the soul of it follower's faith. It may not be easy to understand, but since it is the reason and justification for every act(ion) carried out, almost dictating every move for all living, it is important we try to cognize.

Inshallah. God's Will…*From God everything emanates.* They believe they bring justice and enlightenment and truth and peace, (or their version of), to the Godless world. (This essay is not a theological discussion, I have written other essays about that. But let me bring up one point; If they believe everything emanates from God, then how can anything in this world be Godless? To be more specific, how do *we* the infidels exist?) In my view, theirs belief system is a mad, fanatical doctrine which has brought suffering, death, and chaos to millions of innocent persons. They believe they must take over management of the entire world and conquer all other races and religions. They are taught there is a place in heaven for those whom die killing others. Now just to be fair, not all Muslims follow this doctrine. I have friends whom practice the Islamic faith. I suppose you could compare them to Catholics who do not agree with everything decided in Vatican II. But, having lived in the Middle East and unfortunately observed the extreme actions and behavior which was fueled by the belief of their religion, I stand by the statements written above.

Without directly commenting on our current strategy concerning terrorists, mainly because I am no longer involved and have no idea what the actual strategy is, (if you think reading the newspaper or watching the news will give you all of the information, well, no offense, but quite frankly, you are an idiot.), there are, of course, some comments/thoughts I have about any strategy when it comes to dealing with terrorists.

Being a son of the south combined with some of the places I have lived, mosquitos are a species I am very familiar with. I consider terrorists a lot like misquotes. So let me use this knowledge to describe terrorists; think of terrorists like mosquitos. You don't kill mosquitos by going to a picnic, or into a swamp waiting for the mosquitos come out and then get sharpshooters to kill them one at a time. You kill mosquitos by identifying where they are in the swamp or picnic grounds and completely wipe them out, unfortunately along with most other insects in the area. But that is how you rid yourself of them. Terrorists are mosquitos. Pick your method, swat away or enjoy your picnic. Sorry, but those are your options. Now before you tell me my logic is flawed and ask why are we having a picnic in a swamp to begin with, I have an essay on that as well. For the point of this essay, it doesn't matter if we agree with our government's choice of picnic locations, the fact is we are there.

Okay, let me go back to Russia for a moment. (Actually I would like to go back to Russia.) Because of certain media reports many people are under the impression the majority of Russians are oppressed and dissatisfied with their President. This is not the case. When Putin invaded and took back Crimea, his popularity among the Russian People reached heights which some may compare to Peter The Great and his popularity during his reign. Of course it is true, Russian citizens have complaints concerning government policies within the country proper, but we must remember, these are a people who lived under a State created by Stalin. Speaking of Stalin and his comparison to the current Russian leader; Putin has consolidated governmental power and his authority. This means he will most likely be President of Russia for the rest of his life.

To Be Continued or Stand-by

TICKET TO RIDE

Besides being an excellent song by The Beatles, is also how I view organized religion. Stay with me here. There have been many occasions when I am asked how I consider myself a practicing Catholic when I disagree with so much of the Catechism as I do; the simple answer is because I choose to.

Let me ask you a question, if you believe in God or a Higher Being, would it be safe to say that you believe on some level that Entity created all the trees in this world? For the sake of this essay, let us just say, *yes*. Okay, so there are oak trees and there are pine trees. There are apple trees and banana, (wait, banana trees are actually bushes), and orange trees. There are a lot of different trees okay. Now, are any of those trees any more of a tree than the rest? For the sake of this essay, let us just say, *no*. Now, if God created all these different type of trees, which are all trees, perhaps He created or allowed or whatever, all of the different religions, denominations, faith-based systems of worship or learning to exist so every person could understand God in their own way; in a way that made/makes sense to them, personally. Could more one than one religion be true? Now let me make it clear that I am not a pluralist, believing all religions are basically the same and equally a means to salvation. In fact, there are issues I have with all organized religions. As far as I can tell, you do not get to heaven on a bus or in a group. It is a personal journey *you* undertake.

You are your own ticket to ride and that ticket is your Faith with religion being your vehicle. Faith is personal and we each view it, take it, or leave it on our own. So who is to say what organized religion is more Holy than another; certainly not another human. Never, have I heard or read anything about facing judgement by God with a committee or in a group; you face it on your own.

Faith, I have always understood to be created by God, and religion created by man. Considering the bang-up job man has done with everything else we have created, religion is bound to be flawed. But Faith, it may just be pure. Of course this is with the understanding of people's desires often influence what they believe; or as Demosthenes, the Greek Orator noted, *"What a man wishes, he generally believes to be true."* No this essay is not going to discuss truth; let us just stick with Faith and beliefs...still with me?

Terrific, you are still here? Buckle-up!

Due to my writing, speeches, and lectures, my religious views are very well known; hopefully it shows that my interests in epistemology is not solely circumscribed to spiritual questions, but also cerebral ones...(*not solely/soul(y) limited*) The example of the trees above with regards to organized religions is not to suggest I subscribe to Universal Salvation or Pluralism.

Oh, within epistemology, with regards to Christianity philosophy, there are four main doctrines:

- Universal Salvation
- Pluralism
- Inclusivism
- Exclusivism

Each one of these religious doctrines, when taken separately, include points which taken logically, makes sense, and depending upon which organized religion you practice, seem to have cardinal virtue.

Just to be clear, I am not endorsing any of them.

The main debate amongst Christian theologians is the difference between Inclusivism and Exclusivism. The basic view of most conservative Christian religions and Islam, (No! I Am Not Equating Conservative Christians With Muslims!), is Exclusivism; the view there is only one true religion and you can only be saved by accepting that religion. Other Christian religions subscribe to Inclusivism; that there is only one true religion but that it is possible for people to be saved by that religion without consciously or explicitly belonging to it.

What do I believe? I believe you will find what you truly seek...even if you do not understand what it is you are seeking. For me, it is a ticket to salvation.

Amen

HOT FOR THE TEACHER

There is a ninety mile an hour song…a song that is best listened to while driving over 90 MPH. Yes, I do have a ninety-miles-per-hour-music-playlist. Perhaps I'll share it, someday. For now, let us keep our eyes front and sit up straight. Teachers, let us hear it for them, seriously. We trust them with our babies for God's sake; we should take care of them or at the very least acknowledge them, since we as a society have decided to pay them…um… Do you know the average starting salary for a teacher is? Not much. If your only knowledge of teachers stims only from your time in school you may not be aware of everything they are required to do and everything they actually do.

My understanding of teachers is a bit more personal. Aside from dating teachers in California during my late twenties, I have been a student for much longer than I have been anything else. My Mother Linda was an elementary school teacher. Her father was a Professor at Appalachian State University. My Grandmother Mary was a school teacher. Through all of their eyes I was able to catch a glimpse of their working world and what it consisted of. (Not Grandmother Mary's eyes; I think she was legally blind before she was legally blind.)

As a parent it became more obvious to me how important teachers are and how much they actually do. Listen, if they are dealing with me, and I am only one parent, *wow*, I cannot imagine dealing with me, plus twenty to thirty more "me-s". (Because I am writing praises about you, teachers, I expect to receive a pass on grammatical and spelling errors…Please, save your exegesis and e-mails…)

Teachers are more than educators. Professors are educators. Teachers are that plus, care givers, first responders and more. My daughter has a peanut and tree nut allergy which is quite severe. This requires her teachers to be even more diligent, because of her, one student. Who knows what the other students have going on? Anyone who has been a leader in any capacity knows how stressful it can be to focus your team towards a certain goal or direction. Within a team's individual personalities, skill sets and limitations, you, as a leader, maximize strengths, back up weakness, and are constantly refocusing/changing as you march to your goal. Now, imagine having that same mission, with a team of, um, twenty, 27, okay twenty-five, and not only do you have a goal to reach but you must also instruct the team how to do what they need to do and more.

The peanut allergy alone has doubled in recent years. Guess who is responsible for all of these children? Yup, teachers. For those of us who have children, aren't our babies the most important thing to us? If you were to give me the option to focus all my energy on one thing and just to keep it simple, that list consisted of, sex, beer, poker, cigars and my children…I would choose my children every time…unfortunately. (Oh, come on, let's face it, I have better offers on the table, and I just listed them; but that is what love does to you.) We love our children. Okay, getting back. So for around 40k we ask teachers to teach, monitor, secure, and even police our children. On top of that, I have personally seen my children's teachers cleaning toilets and disinfecting toys. But there is more.

Let's see, on average teachers have a sixty-five hour work week. On top of reading, writing, and arithmetic (why was it ever called the 3 R's?), you have sex education, health care and the most popular, standardized tests. School's mandates require these tests to receive funding. It is ridiculous. Wait, I'm not finished.

Teachers also meet with parents like me. (That alone should bump their salary up into the next tax bracket, because I am a pain in the ass, and even more so when it come to my children.) They supervise fire drills, safety procedures, eating habits, extracurricular activities, go on school trips. They must be CPR and First Aid certified, (which requires re-certification every, whenever…another eight hours gone.), and dollars to donuts they would most likely pass any food sanitation inspection from the FDA. Um, overextended? Maybe. Does the name Custer mean anything to you?

May I Be Excused

COLUMBUS DAY

A little bit of housekeeping before we get started. First of all his name was Cristoforo Colombo. For the remainder of this essay Cristoforo Colombo will be referred to as C.C. (If that made you think of the lead guitarist of the awesome hair band Poison, you just dated yourself, and impressed me. We are going to get along just fine.) This essay will only focus on the actual voyages and what was found that was previously unknown to Europe. Now, before anyone starts *sharp-shooting* at me with statements such as, *"How could C.C. discover a continent which already had inhabitants? The Caribbean and South America were not lost; people lived there.",* consider the following, which I am able to articulate because something along those lines has been brought to my attention or asked at every lecture and book reading I have given this past year.

First, to quote the comedian/actor Eddie Izzard,
"Do you have a flag? No flag, no country..."

Regardless of the indigenous inhabitants, no one in Europe was aware of any territory between them (Europe) and Asia. Not the cartographers, not the clergy, not the scientist, not any of the monarchs, nor the sailors.

"What about the Vikings and Leaf Erickson?"

Hold it! Hold it! I'll get there. But for now understand that yes they found, established a settlement, and then never returned or mentioned anything about it after one year. Didn't record it, didn't write a song about, didn't exploit it, didn't care about, and didn't even include it in their oral history. Like having sexual intercourse with a less than fetching person while on summer vacation with your parents the year before you leave for college, some things you just choose not to share with everyone.

C.C. arrived to a place not represented on any map/chart, places unknown. When he arrived, C.C. discovered a new place and when he returned to Spain he shared his findings. Doesn't matter if he was in the wrong place; no one knew the difference. Let me present this scenario to you;

You are driving one day and get hungry. Looking for a place to eat you spot a small mom & pop restaurant. You had no previous knowledge of the establishment. It is lunch time and a lot of people are dining in this establishment. You go in, find a table and eat. As you are leaving you think of how satisfying the meal was. Later that evening, would you be incorrect telling someone, "I discovered this terrific little restaurant today. We should go there for lunch." (If you want to replace discovered with found, go ahead.) My point is this; obviously other people knew it was there, but you didn't. Nor did anyone at your home know of that restaurant. So it would be natural to share with whomever what you found/discovered, whatever. Is that about as clear as a glass of muddy water?

Okay, what about archeologists discovering cave paintings; are you going to tell me they were not discovered because people had already been there and *tagged* the walls to prove it? Moving on…

This essay will not get into why C.C. is described and portrayed to be so vile that Stalin won't sit at Old Scratch's lunch table with him in the ninth circle of hell. Honestly, you would not be mistaken to have the idea that C.C. was more evil than a Nazi-Vampire-Star-Wars-Storm-Trooper-Zombie-On-A-Mission-To-Kill-Blind-Kittens-On-Easter-Sunday.

The chart C.C. used during his audience with King Ferdinand and Queen Isabelle was created in 1491 by German cartographer Henricus Martellus. While this chart was widely accepted to be the most accurate of the day, it was not error-free. The Earth and its dimensions were represented with the wrong projection. (If you do not understand *map projection*, look it up; it has to do with representing a round object on a flat surface.) The chart used, while not reducing the circumference of the third rock from the Sun, depicted land masses to be greater than they were and bodies of water to be much smaller than they actually were.

When C.C.'s expedition made landfall on October 12, 1492, they had sailed roughly the same distance the Martellus Chart (map) depicted as the distance between Europe and sɪ'pæŋgəʊ (Japan). Because of this, C.C. speculated they landed on one of the small islands believed to be off the coast of Japan, meaning Japan proper should be located in the general area. C.C. immediately sent an expedition commenced to find it, Japan.

Facts

- The circumference of the Earth was an established fact.
- North was not depicted or shown at the top of maps.
- Maps / charts from this time period clearly establish what was considered to be the known world.
- The islands C.C. found/landed upon/discovered/accidently ran into/ whatever…were not depicted on any know European map or chart.
- C.C. did not think he landed in India. His destination was India but he thought he reached sɪˈpæŋɡəʊ (Japan).
- C.C. did not land in North America.
- C.C. did land in the Caribbean and then South America

An excellent book, *Mapping Paradise,* by Alessandro Scafi is about the search for the Garden of Eden. (The book contains over one-hundred historic maps.) The Garden of Eden, believed to be in the east, was show to be at the top of the world of most maps in 1492. While the circumference of the Earth had been calculated centuries before, no land mass was shown or know to be between Europe and Asia.

When persons state C.C. never set foot in America, they should be referring to North America and more specifically the land mass we know as the U.S.A..It is true, C.C. never set foot in North America. He did land in the Caribbean and then South America, both unknown by Europeans to exist and those lands were never depicted on any map before his voyages. (I know this is a technical nip-pick, because I know what they meant, but there is no way he could have discovered the U.S.A. because um, it didn't exist. No revolution against the British would take place for another three-hundred-and-thirty years. Words and language are fun.)

Okay, just to catch-up:

- 985 A.D. The Vikings set up a colony on Greenland and a camp on In Newfoundland. The camp lasted one year and the colony was abandoned in 1408.

- 1492 - C.C. did not discover North America but he did discover previously unknown islands known today as Cuba and San Salvador which is part of um...
- 1498 - On his third voyage C.C. landed in South America (previously unknown) and named the continent Paria. He still thought he was south east of Asia.
- 1502 – Portugal funded Amerigo Vespucci to map the coast of the new continent C.C. discovered four years earlier...South America

There really is a lot information out there about this subject. In fact, I discovered so many interesting things on the subject I could write a book about it...but would a book about the discoveries I made whilst reading about the discoveries of others be a new book? Screw it, I'll just catch a flight to India.

Fair Winds And Following Seas

HARVEY DENT

By design, life is difficult. "Hold it! Hold it!" Let me change that; Old Scratch's desires our lives to be difficult, going against God's design.

The last thing any of us needs is another person making our existence any more difficult than it already is. I don't know about you, but I have proven myself extremely capable of creating my own problems without the assistance of two-faced friends.

It may be time for you to elevate the type of people you have around you. No, I am not going to get into toxic personalities and people to avoid. (However, you could always check out *Arya's List* if you want to know the people to avoid...) Recently I came across something written I found interesting, *You are the average of the five people you spend the most time with.* Now I am not saying that quote is true because I am not certain how such a declaration could be proven. But it is interesting to think about. It reminded me of how one goes about identifying the mark at the poker table; if you cannot immediately make out the mark, it's you.

As you read this, keep in mind how people in your life behave in certain situations. This is not meant to call people out, nor is it meant to cause you any trouble or start trouble. As I mentioned before, this essay is to make you think. Keep in mind, nothing bad ever came from thinking, except for thinking it was a good idea to utter the phrase, "Hold my beer for a second and watch this..."

You may be surprised to find out some of the people in your life are only in it for themselves. "Wow, James, you really went out of a limb there; what other profound insights are you gonna drop on me?"

Harvey Dent won't support your vision for your life and takes every opportunity to put you down. Real friends will call you out on your B.S.. Which is good and we all need people we trust to give it to us straight. But the flip side of that coin is real friends will also support you when you are doing something right. This is probably the best sign to evaluate your relationships. Your friends or loved ones are supposed to know you better than anyone else in the world can. If they do not encourage you to pursue your goals, but instead try to put you down; well, (that's a deep subject), you have got a Harvey Dent as a friend. You already know the type that say things to the tune of, "You can't do it.", and then make fun of or flat out mock your desire to improve yourself and your life or your situation. They usually have at the ready a long list of people who have failed at what you are currently trying to do or have prosed to do. They may subtlety or not say you shouldn't even try and just give up.

Harvey Dent won't man-up and apologize when they are wrong. When someone puts their personal pride over their relationship with you, stop the car and kick them to the side of the road. Real men and classy women know when they are wrong and are strong enough to accept and acknowledge they made a mistake; gentlemen and ladies will take this concept further and apologize for the way they behaved. Real friends, after emotions have cooled, are able to discuss whatever led to an argument or disagreement.

Harvey Dents talk about others behind their back. You can be certain if someone gossips about others to you they gossip about you to others. Real friends do not want to create drama within a closed circle just for entertainment. Gossip for the sake of drama is a clear indication of emotional immaturity. The H.D.'s in this world use gossip willingly to safe guard their own weak self-esteem. They cannot or do not want to improve themselves, so they try to keep everyone else from doing so. You needn't worry about these people for long because as you grow personally and professionally, you will eventually leave them behind. They are never leaders and are never the dominate personality within any relationship. You cannot play both sides and be victorious because when a conflict is reconciled only those who have taken a stand, one way or the other are identifiable. You may be the winners or you may be the loser; but Harvey Dents will be forgotten.

The Harvey Dent Hall of Fame Checklist

- They take more than they give. The leeches within any given group
- Someone looking for opportunities to further an agenda at the expense of others or even at the expense of the relationship.
- Someone who keeps score in a relationship is a Dent

- They don't celebrate when you win. (Keep in mind, your personal success provides you with an opportunity to analyze how other people behave towards you.)
- They don't stand up for you. (The knowledge you have another's six and they have yours is the reason warriors return home from battle and the foundation upon societies have been built. This is why betrayal by these back-stabbing s.o.b.s hurts so much. It isn't your friend didn't intervene on your behalf, it is they betrayed the bond and now you are left alone on the battlefield of life. Real friends would risk personal damage to protect a bond/relationship they value.)\
- You are only friends because you have a similar objective, not similar mind-sets.
- They ridicule you in front of others to make themselves look better. (Real friends make fun of each constantly and they have an interesting approach in the way they do it. It is based upon personal knowledge not ridicule. There is a difference.)
- They will tell others your secrets. (Please be careful with whom you confess to...)

Now, Go Flip A Coin.

THOSE LIKE ME

I meant for this to be the first essay of this book
"Only put off until tomorrow what you are willing to die having left
undone" Pablo Diego José Francisco de Paula Juan Nepomuceno María
de los Remedios Cipriano de la Santísima Trinidad Ruiz y Picasso

As people who know me will attest to, I am a procrastinator who's CV's detail my experience and expertise in stalling. Turns out, many authors and writers are people like me. In the course of starting this particular essay, I have smoked a cigar, smoked a brisket, background checked a babysitter, and watched three Clint Eastwood movies. (A Dirty Harry marathon was on TV, what would you have me do. Granted, it wasn't on TV due to a broadcast and I had to load each of the DVDs to create the *D.H.M* . But that is only because the brisket had to smoke for six hours and I needed a way to keep track of the time.) So as you can see I am a highly motivated individual.

This of course doesn't mean what you are reading is not important or meaningful. It just means I was thinking of many other things before actually sitting down to write this. That is not entirely true. I have recently positioned my writing space above a chest-of-drawers which allows me to stand while writing; this makes it easier for me to walk away from what I am doing. Yes, I am taking procrastinating to an entirely new level. For instance, this book has been under contract since 2015.

There are many reasons people put off doing what they know they need to accomplish. Many of the people who do this were very good in school. I was good in school, even if I didn't have the best grades. Early on I realized I could maintain a B average with minimal effort. Always scored an A in English though, even if I did all of the work at the last minute. Reading was something I enjoyed and plowed through books above my level in grade school, where other students read haltingly. Because of this, I learned a very bad lesson; success was achievable upon my natural talent. Now, this may have been true in school, but not so much in the actual world. In life a lot of people have talent and a lot of people make a living doing work that has nothing to do with their talents or what they are good at or even doing something they enjoy. The successful people, those who like what they do, put their God given talents to use. Success can be measured in so many different ways but I will, just this once, keep it simple; if you are happy, you are successful.

There is more to this essay I need to add, but I'll do it later.

That's Enough

ALEXANDER SELKIRK

1709Alexander Selkirk Rescued after Four Years Stranded on a Desert Island

Selkirk was an unruly Scottish sailor who quarreled with his captain and asked to be put ashore on an island in the Pacific in 1705. Which by the way, as a sailor myself, and the son of a son of a sailor, is there any other type of sailor but unruly? I knew a Chief Petty Officer when I was in the Coast Guard who's lifer stripes were red. For those who don't know, if you have gold stripes, you were awarded the Good Conduct Medal every few years. If you had red stripes, you were an out of control but awesome shipmate. The kind of guy you wanted beside you when everything was going wrong…because that guy, a crazy out of control m-f'er would save your life.

Tired of Selkirk's troublemaking, the captain granted him his wish. Selkirk promptly regretted his decision and chased after the boat, but to no avail. He survived on the desert island by eating shellfish and goats. He domesticated feral cats to keep himself safe from rats. When he was rescued four years later, his story became the inspiration for what fictional character? If you think I am going to tell you to look it up, you must know me.

The End

HOW VERONICA SAVED
CHRISTMAS...DINNER

They Are Always Listening

A few years ago we spent the holidays with my sister and her family. It was a great holiday; my three children and her three children and two children my sister took in for the week for a friend meant eight little people were constantly on hand to terrorize the pets, vandalize the neighborhood and create havoc for anyone over the age of thirty. There were plenty of adults on hand as well which provided the time honored tradition of *community babysitting* meaning there were always at least two adults sober enough to ensure the house didn't burn down and/or drive someone to the emergency room. You know, what is a family holiday without a little drama? I'll tell you what that is...boring...a bad movie...and probably a lie.

Every great, entertaining holiday movie revolves around a family with all of the normal shenanigans only a family can bring. All of our families are crazy but that does not make them dysfunctional...it makes them real. I don't know about you, but whenever I am spending time with someone's family and everything is a little too perfect and everyone gets along all the time, I start wondering if there are bodies in the basement or clown suites in crawl spaces. You do not have to worry about that with my family. My family could not agree upon any plan, much less a sinister one; not to mention, even if my family was given a plan to follow, we couldn't do it. Individually, most everyone in my family is successful, hardworking and accomplished. But put members of my family together, to work as a unit, to achieve a common goal...and...well, lets just say that vampires will accomplish more in the daytime than my family working together will...Moving on...

Two of my sister's favorite things are to eat a terrific meal prepared by someone else and attempting to flummox her older brother. This particular Christmas holiday was no exception. On Christmas Eve morning…wait, that doesn't flow…lets try that again; *On the morning of Christmas Eve* (much better) my dear little sister was doing her best impression of a classic Disney Character. She asked me if I would cook Christmas dinner. You may wonder how does that in anyway relate to a classic Disney Character; I will tell you… the next thing she said after springing her last minute request made me think of Bambi's Mother…as in, *This mother isn't gonna make it out of the meadow today.* Obliviously I said no problem and asked her what she had planned. Her reply is why siblings are so great. "Oh, I don't have anything planned so cook whatever you want; the stores are open until four." Bambi's Mother! When she told me I would be cooking for fifteen people, I seriously considered serving venison.

Since I wanted to spend my time with my three heartbeats rather than spend the entire day cooking I decided my Favorite Uncle's tenderloin recipe was the way to go. An elegant, yet simple meal which is always a hit. Now the meal itself is not difficult; but we were at my sister's home which meant everything else would be. Not in a bad way mind you, but more along the lines of *you have got to be kidding me*!

It was time to remove what was destined to be an excellent main course off the grill. I asked my sister where she kept her cooking utensils. She didn't know, she doesn't cook. I asked her where she or her husband kept the BBQ utensils; she looked at me as if I had asked her to explain Quantum Mechanics. What was destined to be the excellent main course of Christmas dinner was approaching five minutes too long on the grill and I was slowly beginning to lose my Christmas cheer. Tearing through my sister's kitchen drawers and cabinets like a first-grade teacher looking for a cigarette on a field-trip, I was starting to worry. That was until I felt a double-tug on my trousers. Looking down I saw my four-year-old darling daughter Veronica looking up at me smiling. One little hand still grasping my slacks and the other trying to hold up a present, which compared to her frame was large. As gently as I could muster I told her I was busy but would open her gift when I was finished cooking. Veronica is very sweet, but being the middle child of an older sister and a baby brother, she has absolutely no problem getting attention when she wants it. There is no, *Marsha, Marsha, Marsha* complex with my Stardust. My attempt to get back to her was met with a cute, but stern, "No Daddy, open this." So I did what any other father does when his daughter wants him to do something…you do it. (Daughters seem to have some sort of superpower over their father.)

The gift my little girl so adamantly wanted me to open was…well, it was from her and her sister to me. It was their big gift to me that Christmas, the one they picked out for me themselves and one they had planned to be the last present I opened that day. My little girl had obviously heard the commotion, understood the conversation between her Aunt and I, and decided on her own to go to the Christmas Tree, find the gift and bring it to me to open. What was behind her smile and under the wrapping paper was a set of BBQ utensils. I absolutely positively love being a Daddy. I had her and her sister come outside to "help" me with the grill like we do at home. That is how Veronica saved Christmas…Dinner…

The End

MY SISTER LESLIE

A Lovely Person A Loving Lady A Mother of Two A Daughter to Three A Granddaughter to Four A Big Sister to One A First Cousin to Two A Little Sister to Two An Aunt to Six A Sister-in-law to Three A Friend to Many A Firebrand A Debutant A Dancer A Bar Tender A Christian An Artist A Homemaker A Caretaker A Faithful Spouse

Leslie was all of this and more.

BELIEVE IN SOMETHING

Belief is important; you can believe that. Belief in oneself is important. Belief in God is important to me. Belief in whatever you decide has merit in your life should be more important than anything others think of you. More important than the way you were raised; more important than where you were brought up; more important than wealth; more important than appearance; more important that talent; more important more important than any given circumstance.

A crises of Faith is a natural occurrence for those of us who have Faith.. From what I have read, every person who values Faith may very well experience this uncomfortable occurrence. It does not make you weak; it does not diminish your beliefs; it is nothing to be ashamed of. According to the Bible, Jesus Christ Himself wept tears of His Own blood while speaking to God in the garden the night before His crucifixion.

"...and when it's Christmas, I do believe in Santa Clause..." Frank Sinatra

The saying, *"A ship in a harbor is safe but that is not what ships are for."*, also speaks to those who face doubt. You never really understand how precious love is until you have lost love and found love again. How much more you value and protect and nurture love this next time is a direct response to your past experience. You never really understand how strong your Faith is until your Faith is challenged. Life is not about how strong you are or how tough you are or how hard you can hit.

Epistemology is the philosophical branch of study dealing with belief and knowledge. Among the fundamental questions are: What is knowledge? Can we absolutely know anything? When is a belief justified? Are any beliefs absolutely certain? Basically, what are the distinctions between believing something to be true and knowing something to be true? To me, it is an interesting field of study. The important thing to remember is a search for truth is not the same thing as an attempt to ensure you never hold any false beliefs. In demanding absolute proof, I am not so much seeking to have the facts presenting before me as much as I am attempting to ensure I am not fooled again. It is true people develop false beliefs because of naivety, but it is also true a person may fail to acquire true beliefs because they are too cynical.

The Trouble With Attempting To Make Yourself Stupider Than You Are Is That You Often Succeed

Our fears can influence our beliefs just as much as our desires can.

"What a man wishes, he generally believes to be true." Demosthenes

You do not need to look far in the world for examples of the above; just think of an overly protective parent believing their child's teacher is treating their child unfairly or a boxing fan belief's about a referee's performance during a fight.

What about spiritual problems some persons face preventing them from seeing what I believe to be the truth about God? Well, (deep subject), this is an easy one which should be able to be cleared up within this short essay…not. For those requiring proof, much of the evidence we have central to the Christian claims about Jesus comes from the testimony cited in the New Testament which are based upon eye witness accounts and near-contemporaries of the time. So, from this perspective, the evidence of Christian truth rests on faith in the credibility of certain human testimony. This faith is not to be confused with spiritual Faith. Faith, I believe, can produce its own evidence. As Kevin Kinghorn wrote, "Sin blinds, and faith opens our hearts and minds to God's gracious presence in our world and in our lives."

What else do I believe? What God promises, God will provide. When nothing is for certain, everything is possible. Feelings are small in comparison to facts and Faith. Every great achievement was once considered impossible. There is a thin line between keeping your chin up and sticking your neck out. Keep your doubts to yourself but share your Faith with others.

Just The Beginning

EVERYTHING WILL WORK OUT

When I was a boy, many a summer was spent with Grandparents on their farm in South Carolina. There was always a lot of work to do, but most of the time I didn't mind. My Granddaddy would take me everywhere he went and taught me how to do everything he was doing. He was a patient man, a man of faith and an excellent teacher. He also loved to tell us stories. It wasn't until many years later I realized the stories I heard had a purpose. Much like Christ and his parables, my Granddaddy's stories contained lessons about life and living. Love, Faith, honor, self-identity, all of these were subjects he spoke about. The stories stuck with me.

Now that I have my own children, I am glad those stories stayed with me, but it wasn't all due to my legendary memory. When I was about fifteen years old my Grandparents came to visit us in South Florida. Every evening after supper during their visit, we would sit on the porch and listen to my Granddaddy tell stories. On the second night, unbeknownst to everyone, I placed a tape recorder under the rocking chair my Granddaddy had claimed as his, and prompted him to tell some of the stories I had first heard as a boy. I still have this cassette tape and am looking forward to sharing it with my children some day in the future when they want to know about their Great-Grandfather. To me, it would be awesome to have them look through old family photographs while listening to the man in the pictures tell stories.

As a practicing Catholic, even when I have doubts, I must believe God has a plan, even if I cannot see it. As a father, it is my responsibility not to show any personal doubts and make certain my children feel safe, loved, and secure in the belief in God and that everything will work out just the way it is meant to. As a parent you smile when you want to cry and project positivity regardless of how you feel inside. You cowboy up with your weapons drawn and you move forward…you do it for your children. Thank goodness my arsenal contains stories from my childhood.

We all go through life's ups and downs, living in the space between things are terrific and things are awful. Blessings in disguise and clouds with a silver lining are concepts I loathe. The grass is greener, sour grapes, half-filled or half-empty glasses and lemons to lemonade; what a crock when you are hurting. Find me in a certain mood and I say, *"get off my lawn"*, *"this is the pits"*, *"who the hell been drinking out of my glass"* and I'll tell you what to do when life gives you lemons, pick'em up and throw them at people. (Speaking of lemons, why is it lemon liquid dish soap contains real lemon juice but lemonade contains artificial flavoring?) However, if you catch me in a good mood; I realize good things may lead to bad things. Bad things may lead to good things. If you are peace with this fact, you may have some serenity.

Storytime:

There is an old man who owns a prize thoroughbred horse and one afternoon it runs away. The old man's friend stops by to express his condolences. The old man says, "Don't know if it's good or bad, but God has a plan." The friend is surprised the old man is not upset. Later that evening, the prize thoroughbred returns with twelve wild stallions. Upon learning the news, the old man's friend states, "Wow, now you are rich with horses. Your problems are over." The old man said, "Don't know if it is good or bad, but God has a plan." Next morning the old man's son is thrown while trying to break one of the stallions, causing a compound fracture to his left leg. The old man's friend hears about the accident and expresses sympathies. The old man says, "Don't know if it is a good or bad thing, but God has a plan." Two days later, the army passes through with orders to conscript all able-bodied young men whom will then be shipped off to war. The old man's son was spared and his friend says….

Quit Worrying

ACROSS THE BOARD

Zero tolerance policies and practices are more harmful and dangerous than people realize. Also, one of the reasons zero tolerance policies and mandatory prison sentence guidelines were adopted in the first place is disgusting to begin with…but I will go into depth about privatization of prisons and other municipal services in another essay. But for the moment, consider who(m) benefits from mandatory maximum prison sentences? For now, here is an example about zero tolerance policies.

When I was a teenager in South Florida with a driver's license, a fast car, and the common sense of a monkey, the vertical pedal on the right was often in close proximity to the floor board. Naturally I was pulled over for speeding more than once. I received my share of lectures from a cop and even had one policeman call my Step-Dad which resulted in my car being parked for a week or so. I went on to school, then the military, then the Federal Government, in many capacities, all of which required a security clearance. It would be nice to believe I did my part making the world a safer place, perhaps we did. But this is the thing, if any of the zero tolerance policies regarding moving violations or speeding which exist today were in place when I was under the age of eighteen, I would not have been able to do anything I just mentioned other than go to school. You see, now, if you are pulled for speeding, fifteen miles over the speed limit is considered *reckless driving* and that is a criminal violation. Now before you say, "and it should be…that is crazy fast.", ask yourself this; have you ever caught yourself driving along, five miles over the posted limit only to suddenly realize the posted limit has been reduced because of a *speed zone,* be it, construction or school or workers present, whatever the posted limit was dropped from 45 to 25…guess what, if you are doing fifty and suddenly find yourself in a 25 mile per hour speed zone, you are going double the speed limit which means you are going to jail! (Yep, fifteen, twenty miles over the limit is reckless driving; double the limit and you are in handcuffs.) Now, most of us have had the benefit of being pulled over by an officer who had discretion on how whatever the violation may have been was going to be handled. Well, thanks to body cameras, dash cameras, cell phone cameras and zero tolerance policies officers no longer have the discretion to take circumstances into consideration, to run your license and find that you have never received a ticket, so this is not going to be your first...whatever.

Now for something that I and maybe you have done and gotten away with, a teenager today, sixteen, seventeen years old with no previous issues or problems will now have a criminal record that will follow them for the rest of their life...and that can prevent you from being able to join the military and will prevent you from certain government jobs. This is not a joke. While these policies may have good intentions, they can ruin lives. It concerns me when the potential damage outweighs the intended purpose and it bothers me when these points are raised and nothing is changed.

Zero tolerance policies are lazy, harmful and dangerous. Giving a hug in a school zone is not sexual assault and quite frankly, calling it sexual assault only desensitizes people to the term and what a horror sexual assault actually is. All of us need to be very careful about how we label and describe certain actions.

Now before anyone starts writing their letter to me about how I am calling teenagers caught speeding victims of a system and placing them into the same category as rape victims; stop! No, I am not! That is my point; the generalization of zero tolerance policies, mandatory punishment guidelines, me too movements, all of it...all of us need to pump the brakes for a moment.

Circumstances matter; actual actions matter; intent matters; results of actions regardless of intent matter. But all of these need to be address individually. When it comes to people being hurt; either hurt by the laws or hurt by the lawless, I want to hear what happened. I don't want statistics. Tell me what took place. Show me the damage. Give me our options; options to help, options to prevent, and if need be, options to punish.

Who; What; When; Where; Why. These were the questions which were once asked and answered. Yes, these questions are time consuming and yes these questions are often difficult; but if the situation involved your child, or your spouse, or your parent, or your sibling wouldn't you want those questions asked and answered? If that is the case, then why do we accept less for everyone else? Zero tolerance and mandated punishments only asks one question; what. As far as I am concerned, one question is not enough.

Do we really want to live in a society that creates criminals and belittles victims? Those whom are hurt matter. We cannot seriously help, punish, judge, prevent any of this with a one-size-fits-all regulation or policy. If everyone is a victim, no one is a victim.

That's Enough

OTHER THINGS I WANT MY CHILDREN TO KNOW

I. Give people more than they expect...even when it comes to an ass-kicking **II.** Do not believe everything you hear...regardless of the source; politicians, clergy, teachers, friends, lovers, foes, colleagues, family...yes including your parents which includes me. **III.** Do not spend all you have... but do not keep all you have. **IV.** Do not sleep all you want...but do not rob yourself of rest; even God rested on the seventh day. **V.** "I love you too." should never be an automatic response...if someone tells you they love you, thank them...if you want to express your love for another, look the person in the eyes and tell them...if they give you anatomic response, explain you did not say it to hear it back, you said it so they would know how you were feeling at this moment...if you don't feel love at that moment, do not say it, it would be untrue. **VI.** When you say "I'm sorry", mean it...do not automatically apologize; if you meant to do or say whatever you may have done or said, recognize you are not sorry for your action; but you can still have remorse for the result. **VII.** Believe in love at first sight. **VIII.** Know that other people may not express love in the same way you do; this does not mean they do not love you. **IX.** If your lover treats you poorly, believe them...and be prepared to leave them **X.** Never laugh at anyone's dreams... do not associate with anyone who laughs at yours...no matter whom it may be...family does not get a pass simply because they are your family... if anything, expect more from your family because they are your family. **XI.** Love deeply and passionately...but do not love someone for whom they should be. **XII.** You can stay in a relationship for what it is and sometimes for what is isn't; but never stay in a relationship for what is should be ...any relationship; professional, social, intimate, casual. **XIII.** Don't judge people by their relatives...**XIV.** If someone asks you a question you do not want to answer, ask them "why do you want to know?" **XV.** Any choice you are forced to make is not a choice; it is a test. **XVI.** Do not be afraid to ask someone if the letters *F O* mean anything to them **XVII.** Memorize your favorite poem. **XVIII.** Know your significant other's favorite poem...if they do not have one, write one for them **XIX.** In disagreements, no name calling...it is the only way you may demand the same from another. **XX.** Say "bless you" when you hear someone sneeze...say "thank you" if someone blesses you. **XXI.** When you lose, keep your chin up. **XXII.** When you win, it is perfectly okay to have pride...**XXIII.** Remember, pride, is one of the 7 deadly sins so be careful.. **XXIV.** Don't let little disputes ruin great friendships...**XXV.** Do not let friends take advantage of you, betray you, or disrespect you just because you think they are great **XXVI.** People may change, let them and be prepared to leave them. **XXVII.** Smile when you answer the phone, the caller will hear it in your voice **XXVIII.** Read more books. **XXIX.** Read my books. **XXX.** Read your Greatgrandfather's books. **XXXI.** Read your Grandfather's unpublished Western Novel. **XXXII.** Reread books you enjoy; just like movies, books can be like old friends you enjoy visiting. **XXXIII.** Keep old letters for as long as possible. **XXXIV.** Do not get rid of love letters just because the relationship is over...wait a few years; you may find you are glad you kept them. **XXXV.** Keeping photographs and letters of and from a former relationship is no disrespect to a present relationship; it is your past and a part of you...**XXXVI.** If your present partner is threatened by your past, that is their issue, not yours. **XXXVII.** There is no reason for you to be jealous of ghosts. **XXXVIII.** Do all you can to help create a calm, tranquil, harmonious home...even if that means you need to step out for a moment...if you feel like yelling, go outside and whistle. **XXXIX.** Share your knowledge...**XL.** Do not share all of your past. **XLI.** Read between the lines...you are more intuitive than you realize. **XLII.** Be gentle with babies, the elderly, animals, lovers, former lovers, and loved ones. **XLIII.** Remember the best relationship is the one where your love for each other is greater than the need for each other. **XLIV.** Judge your success by what you had to give up in order to get it... **XLV.** Bank account balances are not a real indication of wealth. **XLVI.** As you age, try to buy assets, not liabilities. **XLVII.** There is no equity in automobiles...I love cars you may too but remember cars are a liability not an asset. **XLVIII.** Cooking and love making have a lot in common. **XLIX.** Dance...**L.** The only control you have in life is how your react to other people...that's it. **LI.** Just because you love someone does not mean you are required to like them. **LII.** Do as I say, not s I do...**LIII.** as a parent I can tell you that regardless of the hypocrisy. **LIV.** I love you more than you can possibly imagine...this is a fact you can believe because I could have never imagined how much I love you.

Learn Roman Numerals

DON'T LIKES

- Unfulfilled Hand-shake Deals
- *Harvey Dent's* (Two-face people)
- When people ignore you simply because they owe you money.
- Complaints about the ending of television series
- The series finale of Game of Thrones
- People who yell at children (unless it is to save a child's life, seriously, calm down)
- Me Too Movement (if everybody is a victim, nobody is a victim)
- When others disappoint me
- When I disappoint others
- When I disappoint myself

CIVIL WAR

"Uncompromising differences between the free and slave states over the power of the federal government to prohibit slavery in the territories that had not yet become states."

That is the sentence in my nephew's high school textbook states as the cause of the four year war. One sentence. Of course the same textbook basically cites the colonists sought independence because of a tax imposed upon their breakfast beverage, so consider the source, I guess.

The Confederates had half of the man power of the Union and the war resulted in the largest loss of life in any war the United States has been involved in to date. But that is not what this essay is about.

Is there a possibility the U.S.A. could become that divided again? Of course. There is a chance of anything. But first, how is war defined? Active participation of a government in a military action? A specific number of battle related deaths? An opposing resistance which can be defeated, surrender, or sign an accord? If this is the definition, the war on terror is not a war. The war on drugs was not a war. The cola wars were not a conflict. The battle against poverty, hunger, homelessness, cancer, aids, opioids, are all mislabeled. If you haven't read my essay labels, buckle-up.

Just look at your own social media. Read what your friends are posting and look at the differences. Do you sometimes wonder how can you be friends with persons holding these opposite views? Sure you can because you are intelligent and not afraid of debate and not ruled by your emotions that reduce your actions to that of a petulant child.

Each side is so unwilling to compromise riots have broken out, according to the media. Riots...in today's world, sit-ins are riots and Red Socks fans destroying a city block after winning the World Series is called a celebration. Does anyone use a dictionary anymore? Of course I would imagine many persons *rioting* would not be able to articulate why they are doing what they are doing. Mob mentality is dangerous and we should never forget that. Reign of Terror anyone? (France...look it up.) Public disturbances and violent protests that escalate are a reality. But not every protest is a disturbance, just as most disturbances are not a protest, they are just annoying for those of us with places to go...like to work.

The New Yorker published an article in 2017 title, *Is America Headed For A New Kind Of Civil War?* First, the definition of civil war was the quote which started this essay. I looked it up so you won't have to; you are welcome. Second, as far as a *New Kind of Civil War* please, someone define that for me, because I cannot find a single definition.

Now, I do not consider a war of words on Facebook or Twitter akin to violence in the streets. Furthermore, a divided media is not the result of deeply felt ideology but more about profit and market shares. I do not believe the U.S.A. is at war with itself. *"War is hell, there are no winners." The divide between CNN and FOX, is about money and shouldn't be any more dangerous than the rivalry between the AFL and NFL. It shouldn't be, but the *uninformed* masses are idiots. (Take the second *n* out of the previous word in italics and we have a problem if they start to march.) As far as the current flock of protesters, what they need, other than a point they can articulate, is a shower and a razor for their girlfriends. Seriously, pitching a tent in front of Wall Street is now a protest? They don't even walk there. They call Uber and then ask the police where they can charge their smart-phones to be able to order a pizza.

The opening sentences of the article read as follows; *"how fragile is the Union, our Republic, and a country that has long been considered the world's most stable democracy?"* So many things wrong with that sentence. The U.S.A. is not a democracy. We are not the most stable, but we may be the most powerful. There is a difference. And *most powerful* is subjective, not objective.

There may very well be a time in the future where the divide among the citizens of the U.S.A. may lead to civil unrest. It has happened before but it is not happening now. It seems to me every decade since the 60's has been trying to compare itself to the 60's. First of all, the 60's didn't just happen overnight and there were more than a few issues that culminated into a perfect storm of citizens protesting their government. It was not all about nor only about race. There were many other issues at play and many of those issues started long before Brown vs Board of Education, Roe v Wade and Vietnam. Seriously, look it up and start with the Great Depression okay. Better still, start with the Roaring Twenties. Just read the headlines, you don't even need to read the articles. The soundbites and photos of the 60's didn't just happen. What may come to your mind when you think about the civil unrest of the 60's was helped along by Constitutional amendments, good and bad, an economic depression, socialists programs, three declared wars which ended isolationism and welcomed xenophobia, Frank Sinatra singing alongside Elvis Presley wearing a tuxedo, a Presidential assassination, a military draft, the Heavy-weight Boxing Champion of the World going to jail for refusing the draft, which in the end didn't really mean that much because thirty years later we elected a President who dodged the draft. Now, I realize I just over-simplified a lot of our history as a nation, but this paragraph contains more facts than many of our children's history books.

Do I personally think there will be mass blood shed between the citizens of our country? Personally, no, I do not and I'll tell you why. Because from what I have witnessed throughout my career is an uncanny inability for most people to commit to cause that may cause them harm and an unwillingness of people to place their loved ones in harm's way for a cause. People are simply too selfish and thankfully too lazy. Thank God for that, because it may be the very thing that prevents another war between the citizens of this country of ours.

Seriously, think about this for a moment; what would it take for you to give up everything you own, sacrifice everyone you love, and leave the entire way you live your everyday life? What would or could possibly push you to do any of those things? Now, before you give an answer think about the people who founded this country of ours; the men and women and their families that went to war against the British for the War of Independence and then think of the men and women and their families who went to war against their own families and neighbors and citizens during the Civil War. Think of how scary that must have been for them. Think of everything they were certain to lose. Think of what a gut-wrenching decision those people made. If you can truly do that and still look me or anyone else in the eye and claim we, you or anyone else in this country of ours, as a whole, faces anything even remotely close to what those people and their families faced, I'm sorry, but you are lying to yourself and everyone else.

Individual atrocities and the evil many people, perhaps even you, face do not turn a society against each other. Let's not take a broadsword to something better dealt with a scalpel. There is a large portion of citizens whom no longer have trust in the federal government, their local government, political leaders, their local law enforcement, and their fellow citizens. What are they doing about it other than venting on social media? It takes more energy to do something positive but it will go a lot further in the long run. You can start in your own neighborhood, hell start in your own home and work outwards. When I was growing up, we had block parties in the apartment complexes and neighborhoods I lived in. Now I have children of my own and we will pull the grill out onto the driveway on a Saturday afternoon and fire it up. Guess what? With no planning and nothing formal we end up with a block party. My children play with their friends while the other parents and adult stand around and bitch about whatever we feel like. Now that is a protest I can get behind and that may be what saves us all.

Post That

CHINA

China where would you rank it among the world powers? Honestly it does not really matter because any list or rank of power or dominance is completely subjective. Depending upon what statistics you use, it is safe to say China has the second or third largest economy in the world. China is the largest exporter in the world. Those facts are insignificant when compared to the following;

China is the largest importer of oil in the entire world.

The fact China has surpassed the U.S.A. as the world's largest oil importer is more significant and disturbing than many realize.

Pop quiz; what do you think would happen if OPEC stopped pricing oil as Dollars per barrel? If you answered, it would be bad, you are correct and also an understatement akin to saying, *from what I've heard, hell might be hot.*

The oil market is the largest commodity market in the world. Please remember that during this election cycle. When any presidential candidate this year makes promises about alternate energies and reducing our dependence on oil, foreign or domestic, they are absolutely positively lying or completely ignorant! Oil does not only power our cars and our homes and light our cities...oil powers the entire world economy. All of those promises are as hollow as anyone who charges for sex...which is the same thing, people get screwed.

Right now, at this moment the U.S. Dollar (USD) is the Reference Currency for the world and it has been since 1944. If you are considering expanding into criminal activity, you are going to be using the USD because it is the only universally accepted currency on the black market, (Think of the urban myth about how the porno industry decided what would be the dominate video format between Betamax and VHS. Yes that it is not entirely true, but you get my point.), and is the most commonly used currency in the international market. Also, most of the world's central banks reserves are held in USD and almost half of all debt issued globally is in USD.

If you are interested in the history of how this came to be, look it up, but here a very brief summary.

Skipping some background, (oh so much background), in 1974, the U.S.A. and Saudi Arabia signed an agreement that all oil purchases would be made with USD. Not just the U.S.A. oil purchases, all oil purchases. Furthermore, the reserves of the money generated from all oil transactions would be channeled through the North American financial system. In 1975 every other OPEC country agreed to do the same. If you somehow fail to grasp how monumental this was/is, please re-read this paragraph, then read it again, have a beverage, kiss your, whomever and read it again. The history of U.S.A. / Saudi Arabia relations, the facts, the cost, what it has cost the U.S.A. and the actual cost will be the subject of another essay.

> In 2019, the Chinese were the world's biggest oil
> importer, surpassing the U.S.A. once again.

The U.S.A. is not, as many of our citizens and politicians believe, China's largest export destination. (It should be no surprise our elected representatives are as ignorant as we are, they are our representatives. Just because a person is elected to office does not automatically make them an expert on every single subject and issue in society. Do you know everything? Then why should they? This annoys me to no end...Jesus Mary Joseph, every time I hear one of our representatives droll on about something I catch myself asking aloud *what does an aneurism feel like?*). Anyway, China's largest export destination is Australia and after the free trade agreement Australia signed with China on 2018 that is unlikely to change. I bring this up because there seems to be this false sense of security that China will not hurt the U.S.A. because doing so would inflict harm upon themselves. Not so much.

So now, the Chinese are the world's biggest oil importer, their largest trading partner (from a profit perspective) is Australia and China holds the majority of U.S.A.'s debt.

Pop quiz; How likely are you to win an argument with your mortgage company if you live in that house?

In my essay *Know Your Enemy* I detailed the differences of military strategy with regards to taking a beach. The Chinese government is currently engaged in a multi effort strategy to change global politics.

China and Russia agreed in 2017 that oil purchases could be made in Yuan. This is now 2020 and the Yuan is an accepted form of payment for oil to not only Russia, but Iran, Venezuela, and Angola. Have you been paying attention to other issues concerning Global Politics, because if not, you should.

In 2018 China announced oil futures contracts would be available in Yuan on the Shanghai International Energy Exchange. This is in now in direct competition with Wall Street oil futures. (Look up how investing in *futures* work...encyclopedia is quicker than the internet, or you can watch the Eddie Murphy movie *Trading Places*...Orange Juice futures were the plot device. I recommend watching the movie because you are going to need some comedy to combat the anxiety all of this should be causing you.) Xi Jinping went one step further with China's entry into the oil futures market by announcing the futures purchased in their market would be backed by gold. This is brilliant! China is now attaching the Yuan to gold, Xi Jinping is stating that when investors sell the oil they purchased with Yuan, the Yuan received as payment will be convertible to gold. Listen, I love my country, but as a private investor with three children whom will probably quit college on me too, I implore the U.S.A. to do something similar. I am a gambler and investing in futures is a risk investment, but this action reduces the risk to a level even our parents would consider even if they don't want to bet against the U.SA. Oh but it gets better, as in *worse,* so much worse.

Pop quiz; What does purchasing oil for Yuan mean with regards to Global Security?

I'll begin the answer by asking another question; what is and has been the preferred method of the U.S.A. to deal with our enemies (describe them how you want, but let's call them what they are)? Sanctions anyone...U.S.A. led UN sanctions. By being able to purchase oil for Yuan, countries, governments, entities, institutions, persons, whomever, purchasing oil in Chinese Yuan can avoid U.S.A. led and U.N. enforced sanctions. If that isn't scary enough, the more investors invest in oil with Chinese currency, the more they are investing in China proper. That means real estate, research and development, technology, infrastructure. It is basically investing in the very future of China.

Okay, back to the second, (but most important), question I asked in this essay; what do you think would happen if OPEC stopped pricing oil as Dollars per barrel? If Saudi Arabia begins to accept another currency for even part, *any part*, of oil production, global markets and global political strategy will be completely altered possibly ending the USD importance thus changing U.S.A.'s dominance in the world.

Of course this won't happen overnight, but as I wrote before, China does not storm the beach to take it. They cannot match the U.S.A. militarily in a straight up fight, but why would they want to try such a foolish tactic? Adversaries of the U.S.A. are guilefully seeking to end it's dominance and are doing so without even firing a shot. What good is a military against that?

Watch Your Six!

AN IRISH WARNING

Helpful list of statements one should not make in an Irish Pub

- I am betting against the Celtics
- I am betting against Notre Dame
- Anyone up for a debate concerning religion?
- U2 blows
- Listen up, drinks are on me!
- When did this pub become a gay bar?

MINIMUM WAGE - OUTSOURCING

Anyone who goes around chanting "American jobs for American workers!" is an idiot, because unless you designate what part of the Americas you are chanting about you are basically shouting "Mexicans and Canadians and U.S.A. citizens jobs for Mexican's Canadians and people in the U.S.A.!" Hey, guess what, even though we like to think we own the world because we like to think we control it, Americans mean more than United States Citizens (USC)...Jesus, Mary Joseph, it's like discussing physics with my sisters\'s children..."*Eric, Ethan, you cannot take such an extreme turn in your front wheel drive car at over fifty miles per hour!*"..."*But Uncle James, it totally works on PS2, which is completely based on real life scenarios...*"

This was initially written as two essays. Those who know me know I have no problem repeating myself; especially if it is in the form of an absolutely terrible joke that only I and perhaps two other people find funny; in which case, I will repeat the terrible joke until even those two people are sick of it. This subject/these subjects I do not find funny so here they are together... one time. Besides, most people don't want to hear/read this even one time.

As I have written before that politicians always seem to agree, only the never seem to agree at the same time. When they do agree at the same time, constituents should be scared or at least pay closer attention. In the last election cycle, both Donald Trump and Bernie Sanders held the same position on outsourcing which can be boiled down to *keep American Jobs for American workers.* Outsourcing has been so vilified I do believe the Arch Diocese of Boston is seeking to make it count as a Deadly Sin.

First, will everyone look at a map once in a while and realize the term *American* does not mean *United States Citizen*, no matter how often it is used. (Seriously, a subscription to National Geographic will get you two world maps and at least one map of the U.S.A. a year.) While ending outsourcing would be detrimental to what barely exists of an economy in poor nations, it very well could be terrific for others. The reason these chants by presidential hopefuls resonated in many cities in the U.S.A. is the fact many jobs, especially in the manufacturing sector, are no longer available to USC...citizens who in many cases came from families who held those jobs for generations. Family pride is real. A sense of belonging is real. Hometown pride is real. National pride is real. Mob mentality is real. Real things can be warped into real dangerous things. (FYI-everything in the previous six sentences is how some of the worst acts in history started.) Getting back on target here, many jobs once available in the U.S.A. been moved abroad and are being completed at a fraction of the cost, resulting in greater profits...for companies...that pay taxes...companies made up of people...who pay taxes...

Second, what does outsourcing have to do with minimum wage? So glad I assumed you asked. Take away wage incentives and other cost incentives to move jobs abroad and those jobs will theroyretacly come back to the U.S.A. Why, in theory? Well, the Federal and State and Local governments would need to cut taxes on corporations to make up for the increased labor cost... this and other certain demands made by companies would need to take place before they willingly moved their operations back to a country they fled. (How many expats do you know ever moved back to the country of their birth permanently?) But just remember, many of those jobs have been away for a while and there is not necessarily a ready, trained, able, and willing work force in the U.S.A. to fill them as there once was.

For those industries that cannot be automated, it could result in many jobs and much work available. Ah, automation...we'll get there and so will I in this essay.

Beside wages and low corporate tax other countries could still attract U.S.A. companies in other ways. How about creating more unregulated markets or no labor restrictions? Does that sound evil? Grow up, that is the world we have created.

Depressed yet? Okay, let us talk about minimum wage for a spell...

If you increase the minimum wage, the poor would still be poor. Sorry. Moving on...what? Explain myself...rarely, but in the case, here you go.

An increase in minimum wage would not end poverty. Most persons earning minimum wage are secondary income earners with-in their household; teenagers with a part-time job or spouses looking to do something with their spare time once children have entered secondary school. The majority of workers either make more than the minimum wage already but do not work or not scheduled enough hours or simply do not work at all.

More Robots; According to an article in the Economist, the most certain outcome of a major increase of minimum wage would be an increase in automation. The only thing that keeps many low paying repetitive simple jobs in the *hands* of people is the up-front cost of installing robots/machines. It is simply too expensive. However, should it become more cost effective and economical, say do to a significant mandated wage increase,...*Hello Hal!...*

Let us not forget the fact machines really suck at certain types of work (insert picture of a vacuum here).

Persons seeking work would flood into areas which could afford the wage increase from everywhere else that could not. Does anyone remember how the U.S.A. government screwed over Puerto Rico? Not that time, the other time. No, not that time either, the other time. No? Okay, I'll just tell you; when Puerto Rico became a territory of the U.S.A. some yahoos thought it would be great to have the poor island subject to the minimum wage of the U.S.A. This mandated wage increase did not improve the quality of life on the poor, (Did I mention poor?), island...employers couldn't afford it. Unemployment on the island increased and migration from the island to the mainland exploded.

Small business. Thank goodness Obama Care, (which could on technical merits alone be called Nixon Health Care), demonstrated the undesired results of major federal government mandate's detrimental effects upon small businesses....

A collapse of small business across the country does not lead to innovation...well, it may, but not the positive type. Most persons will tell you they value small business and believe they are a basic fabric in the national character of the U.S.A. Okay, but let me ask you, this morning, did you get your coffee from a Starbucks, Dunkin Donuts or from a *mom & pop* business? And if you even being to say *I don't drink cof...*,you know the point I was trying to make. If you want to increase the minimum wage, say adios to choices and enjoy calling your small coffee a *Tall* forever. Maybe this won't happen, I don't know and quite frankly neither does anybody else.

Okay there is more. HBO's Game of Thrones did more than allow those who played Dungeons & Dragons in high school to finally be able to experience what a vagina feels like; it also explained how to avoid federal government mandates concerning employees. *Sell-swords* aka, freelancers (Sir Lancelot), aka contactors, aka 10-99 employees. Does your place of employment take in unpaid interns over the summer? Why not, our federal government does?

Have you or anyone you have worked with wanted a promotion, so then took on extra-responsibilities for a period of time without it increasing you salary or rank? What else? Um, anyone at your place of employment, "not on the books"? Of course not, that would be illegal. I should know because I worked for the Federal Government for over twenty-three years. If I were to have had someone working for me and didn't report it, well, let me tell you…that would have been just fine…and it was…So please, politicians, leaders, community organizers, clergy, laymen, and everyone else; spare me any self-righteousness and pander for whatever it is you are seeking elsewhere because I am busy trying to sell my books.

A mandated increase in minimum wage might create an increase racism, xenophobia…but what about the positive? Is there anything positive which could result from an increase in the minimum age? Yes. Simply put, more money earned, more money spent. More money spent, more economic growth. This is of course in a capitalist economy. So if we don't regulate ourselves from existing as a capitalist economy any eleventh-grade high school student passing economics should be able to explain to you a capitalist economy relies upon the notion of workers using their earned income to purchase services and good they do not need to live. Wants vs Needs are the building blocks of growth. They inflate the amount people are able to spend on entertainment and leisure without requiring them to cut back on necessities. This leads to economic growth.

Here is another way to explain it: More money equals more spending; More spending equals more pleasure; More pleasure, more sex. More sex; more people. More people, more workers; More workers, more earners; More earners, more money; More money, more spending; More spending, more pleasure…and so on.

No, I am not equating spending money with pleasure…well, I am, but, ah damn it all down. If we are going to revert to logic, perhaps we shouldn't chit-chat…I mean no one else seems to use logic. What makes you and I so special? Exactly.

That's Enough

WORCESTERSHIRE SAUCE

"Steak Sauce" As my three young children refer to it at home, has always been a major ingredient and condiment in every home of my side of a very large and extended family. It would not be much of an exaggeration to say we put it on or in just about everything except Key Lime Pie and peach cobbler. (*Pop quiz for those non-Floridian natives reading; What is the color of Key Lime Pie?*) At seven, five, and three years of age, my children were already asking for it, (Worcestershire sauce, *steak* sauce, on their rice and mashed potatoes...that is if they weren't already in the process of pouring the bottle themselves. (The necessity to help my youngest and closely monitor my oldest [who's pour was very long...kinda like a well tipped bartender, she had a four second count] was not so long ago. The youngest no longer requires my assistance...the need to monitor my oldest still exists.)

My favorite brand is *Lea & Perrins*, which is the original. My close friend Paul Perry disagrees with me on this and insists *Crystal* is the better tasting of the two. There are not many things upon which Paul and I disagree. This is remarkable considering we have known each other for over thirty years. That is a long time to not have many disagreements. However, the lack of disagreements has nothing to do with having the same view on things, it has to do with the fact that I met him when I was in high school and he is the Dad of a friend of mine from art class. The way I was brought up, respect your elders, took hold...so I basically kept my mouth shut concerning my opinions around him up until a couple of years ago. It was not until after he had read my first book and told me, while he didn't agree with everything I wrote, he did enjoy reading it, did I really begin to open up...a date I suppose he regrets to this very day. (Although, he and his wife Deirdre, along with my favorite Uncle were the persons providing the most encouragement to write a second book...among other things.)

There have been several occasions to which I have challenged Paul as to the better Worcestershire sauce and suggested/threatened to set up a blind taste. But I will never for two, no three reasons, no four reasons:

One: The debate always occurs in his home where he and Deirdre have me over for dinner and a concert. (Paul was in the music business for a while and his knowledge and respect for talent is almost overwhelming...So when he tells me that I should listen to something or come over because there is a concert he would like for me to watch, I do it. He also gives me *homework* which consists of albums for me to listen and be able to discuss with him upon our next meeting.)

Two: The man buys Crystal Worcestershire Sauce by the case...over the internet...Not to mention, if someone asks how he cooked dinner, (yes he is the cook), and it involves Worcestershire, he will give them a bottle when they leave.

Three: Respect your elders...even if they insist you are now on an equal playing field.

Four: Sometimes it is just fun to debate over nothing serious so I have no real desire to settle the issue.

Pass The Sauce

EVERYONE DOES IT

Everyone does it. I most certainly do. Although we won't admit it, this may be the thing that could unite us as humans because every person does, or has at least once partaken in this thing everyone knows about, but no one will ever call you on it once you reach a certain age. In private we acknowledge it may be a shortcoming, but it isn't hurting anyone, so therefore it cannot be a terrible thing. Yet, if exposed, it can make the best of people be viewed in a very different light.

Of course I am writing about mispronouncing words. (What did you think I was writing about? Sinner.) No, I am not referring to non-native English speakers; I am referring to the majority of American English speakers. The fun thing about this is we cannot even blame it on being confused because of speaking other languages. According to a survey I am making up for this essay, only 2 of ten people born into an English speaking family in the United States have studied, (high school Spanish or French does not count), another language. That is awful. Using my own family as an example, I can tell you how awful it is; my children have parents who are able to speak and read another language, yet my only speak English. Why? Laziness. Yep, to lazy to give them a natural head start which would only benefit them in the future.

But yet another downfall of my parenting skills isn't what this essay is about. This is annother, *just for clarification essay*. Below are some commonly mispronounced English words :

HYBERBOLE: There is not a thing called a "hyper-bowl". The word is pronounced, "hy-per-ba-lee"

IRREVERENT: The beginning of this word is supposed to sound like "ear" not "uh".

LIABLE: This is a great court room movie mispronouncement therefore now an actual courtroom mispronounced word. The word actually has three syllables. Therefore it should be "lie-uh-ble", not "lie-bull".

LIBRARY: People like me either drop the first "R" or and a second. But the word should be "lie-brary".

MOOT: It isn't a moot point if you pronounce it "mute" rather than "moo-t"

NUCLEAR: Dennis Miller had a great set about this word on his WHITE comedy album. What ever happened to comedy albums? But basically, "Nuclear" is the type of energy one gets from splitting atoms. "Nucular" is not a word. Sorry to break it to you.

PICTURE: When you are hanging a "picture" do not forget the "c" so it sounds like "pic-tshur". If you are pouring a "pitcher" of beer, drop the "c" before you see me.

POLICE: The thin blue line which protects us all are often called "poh-leece". However the proper way to say the word is "puh-leece"

PREFACE: The first syllable is pronounced "eh", not "ee", so the word sounds like "preh-fehs" not ""pree-face".

SILICON: As in "Silicon Valley". Which is in California. This word should be pronounced "sil-i-con". Not "sil-cone". This is an easy mistake because the latter is used in my favorite surgery, breast implants, which ironically, the most of which occur in the state of California.

SPECIFIC: Sticking with a west coast thing, it is difficult for some to pronounce a "s" before a "p", so some people pronounce this "pacific", which is wrong"

SUPPOESDLY: I am guilty of this one too. Wanting to replace the "D" with a "B" at the end. But *supposedly* the word should be pronounced "suh-pohs-ehd-lee"

TACK: "Tack" sans "t" at the end means "tactic". Whereas "tact" refers to being sensitive in dealing with matters. So be careful of the letter swap.

TRIATHLON: The word only has three syllables, the same as the number of events. Don't be tricked into inserting another "a" in the word.

WHEELBARROW: For some reason, people change "barrow" to "barrel"

fin

HOMONYMS

Another *Just For Clarification* Essay

Two or more words which are pronounced alike, but are both used and spelled differently are called *homonyms*. Below are some common examples:

accede - To comply with. *exceed* - To surpass.
accept – To take, receive. *except* – To exclude.
access – Admittance, admission. *excess* – Surplus.
altar – A place of worship. *alter* – To change.
ascent – Act of rising; motion upward. *assent* - Consent

LIKES

- Falling in love
- Laughing so hard your stomach and face hurts.
- A hot shower.
- Getting mail.
- Taking a drive on a pretty road and going really fast.
- Hearing your favorite song on the radio, while driving on that road, really fast.
- Lying in bed listening to the rain outside.
- Lying in bed listening to the rain outside next to a lovely woman.
- Lying in bed listening to the rain outside next to your children.
- Vanilla milkshakes.
- A long distance phone call. (yes children, before cellular phone, it cost more money to call your grandparents.)
- A beautiful woman taking a bubble bath.
- Your young children taking a bubble bath, for completely different reasons...
- A good conversation.
- Listening to and discussing music with my favorite Uncle Mark
- The beach.
- Finding a 20 bill in your coat from last winter.
- Finding a 100 dollar bill in your tuxedo from your sister-in-law's wedding.
- Laughing at yourself.
- Midnight phone calls that last for hours.
- Running through sprinklers
- Laughing at an inside joke, outside, in front of many people.
- Friends.

- Accidentally overhearing someone say something nice about you.
- Accidentally overhearing someone say something nasty about you, so you can know what those s.o.b.s really think.
- Waking up and realizing you still have a few hours left to put the moves on your girl...because we all know I'm a better agent if I get some in the morning.
- Your first kiss.
- Every kiss after.
- Brushing the hair of your toddler daughter. Pure heaven. Especially when she asks you not to stop.
- Swinging on swings.
- Wrapping presents under the Christmas tree
- Song lyrics printed inside your new CD so you can sing along without feeling stupid.
- Going to a really good concert.
- Making eye contact with a beautiful stranger.
- Winning a really competitive game.
- WINNING
- Remembering time spent with friends who have passed away
- Seeing smiles and hearing laughter from your friends.
- Holding hands with someone you care about.
- Running into an old friend and realizing that some things, good or bad, never change.
- Riding a roller coaster over and over. (The first roller I road was with my father, THE SCORPIAN at Busch Gardens in Tampa Florida.)
- Realizing you have become the character in the Police song, Man In A Suitcase.
- Watching the sunrise as it rises over the dashboard of your car next to your lover.

Two Minute Drill

Okay, two minutes left on the play-clock of your
life. Which two minute drill will you run?

Flee Flicker

Play High-School Football; Attend College; Watch College Football As
The 12ᵗʰ Man; Land A Job; Get Married; Buy A House; Start A Family;
Watch Pro-Football; Earn More Money; Take A Holiday; Watch Son Play
Football; Stay In Shape; Stay In Love; Age Gracefully; Play Touch Football

Hail Mary

Play Football – College –Job – Wife –Children – etc – Turn 30 – Get
Behind – Work Harder – Miss Dinner – Miss Daughter's Recital – Miss
Old Friends – Turn 40 – Get Desperate – Miss Sex – Miss Your Dad –
Miss The Point – Work Harder Still – Play Golf – Play Around – Play
Fake Everything Is Fine – Lose Your Wife, Family, Sanity – Suffer
Heart attack – Suffer Heartbreak – Suffer Stroke – Die Alone

Where You Stand Depends Upon Where You Sit

One Man's Hero - Another Man's Terrorist

BRAVE - SUICIDAL
DETERMINED - PIG HEADED
FAITHFUL - TO YOURSELF

FIELD OF DREAMS

Following my dreams, I'm tired of it and think I just catch up with them later. At the moment there are more pressing matters for me to attend to. If you want to do something, then go do it. So you want to be a writer? Then write. You do not need a piece of paper from an institution to state you are now qualified to be a writer. Just go write something. If people read it, great! You are now a writer. I just saved you 60K a year on a journalism degree. You may send me a check made payable to James Sitton at JS Productions. My children thank you for your donation to the Sitton Family Scholarship Fund.

Mr. Tim Mogilka was my Mass Media teacher in high school. We studied film, mass media, and production. A truly gifted artist himself, he inspired his students to produce whatever they could think of. And we did. We made movies, videos, teen news broadcasts. We could go to Mr. Mogilka with an idea and he would let us run with it. Because of that freedom, we created a lot of work under Mighty Mo's Direction. We filmed off campus, once at an Indian Reservations with Native Americans. (I know that doesn't seem right, but how else would you say it? Even the casinos are called *Indian Casinos* not Native....)

On one particular project, we were able to film a live Florida Panther in it's *natural as could be environment* with the assistance of some Seminole Indians. It was pretty awesome and quite an adventure at 17 years old. All of these and other experiences shaped me into the person I am today. Everything really does work out I the end and yes, God has a plan; even if we cannot see it.

When I was in school, all I wanted to do when I grew up was to write, direct, be involved in film and art. Guess what? It took me 23 years, but that is exactly what I am doing now in my forties. After a brief 23 year segue of government work and bad decisions, I'm here. So, do whatever you want. Make it happen. Pray for guidance, and follow said guidance (not always my strongest virtue)…and enjoy your life. It is truly a gift from God. Use your gifts.

The End

ANOTHER ESSAY ABOUT
ELECTRONIC LEASHES

"As smoking gives us something to do with our hands when
we aren't using them; times gives us something to do with our
minds when we aren't thinking" –Dwight Mac Donald

So smoking is not as popular as it was in 1957 but our hands and minds have plenty to do. It might be suggested we replaced a vice with something more addictive, more expensive, and possibly more dangerous. Of course I am talking about our smartphones. Yes, they could be more dangerous than smoking...if you are driving or if you sent that text while still angry, dangerous! No, smartphones did not actually replace smoking.

Addictive, indeed; seriously, leave your phone at home one day a see how you feel in a few hours. You will feel just fine, because you won't be able to leave your house without your phone. Besides, it probably starts your car and has replaced your check-card.

Not having something to do apparently is a major problem now. Being bored is not an option for most of us. Our parents wouldn't stand for it, we don't like it, and our children could go through life without experiencing it. Being bored, I'm talking about being bored. For most people my age, being bored as an adolescent was a right/rite of passage. Fourteen hour car trips with your siblings in the back of a station wagon, with the luggage and blankets and pillows that made it hotter than......, falling asleep with chewing gum in your mouth, waking up needing the restroom only to be told you slept through the last stop and your father is making 'good time' so here is a bottle. All of this before the Walkman was available; so all you could do was ask 'are we there yet' and pick on your siblings by dividing the back of the car territory into a system more convoluted than any congressional voting re-districting.

As my children got older a new rule was established in the Sitton House, "no screen time during meal time", sporting events, concerts, and family movie nights are not affected by this rule.

Texting while driving is now illegal. Know what is one-hundred percent legal? Writing a letter long hand while driving…

THAT'S ENOUGH

IT'S ON THE LIST

With everything which has occurred in the years since my last book, one would think I have learned quite a bit. This is so very much not the case. Below is a list of things I should know by now, and things I am still working on, things I have come to terms with, and a few things I have learned.

- I'm stubborn, irascible, and loyal.
- Try saying the name "Martha" if someone is trying to kill you.
- You cannot plug a hole with a ring.
- You can believe half of what you see, less of what you hear, and even less of what you know and still be wrong.
- The rain in Spain falls mostly on Spaniards.
- The most effective verbal response is often no verbal response.
- Having a child fall asleep in your arms is one of the most peaceful feelings in the world.
- Being kind is more difficult than being right.
- Never say no to a child who wants to show you something important to them.
- You can always pray for someone when there is nothing else you are able to do.
- Two things I want from a woman besides sex; to laugh with her and to hold her hand.
- I loved the family walks we took after dinner on summer evenings when I was a child.
- Ignoring the facts does not change them.
- There are few moments as peaceful as watching your children sleep.
- Even the ones you fall in love with are not perfect.
- I should show and tell those I love, I love them more often.

- After holding my children for the first time I was theirs for life.
- It is taking me a lot more time than anticipated to become the man I want to be.
- You can keep going long after you think cannot and much longer than you want to.
- Heroes are the people who do what is needed regardless of the consequences.
- There is no such thing as a best friend. There are people you can trust and whom are loyal and there is everyone else.
- Sometimes the one you would take a bullet for is holding the gun.
- I have the right to be angry, but not the right to be cruel.
- Just because someone doesn't love you the way you want them to doesn't mean they don't love you.
- Forgiving yourself is more difficult than forgiving others.
- I am not as forgiving as I would like to be.
- Our background and experiences may influence our personalities, but we are responsible for who we become and how we behave.
- Just because people argue, it doesn't mean they don't have respect for you and just because they don't argue doesn't mean they do.
- You shouldn't be so eager to find out a secret; It could change your life forever.
- When a friend cries out for help, a friend will find the strength to help.
- Titles and status do not make you a decent human being.
- People you care about are taken away too soon.
- The true currency in the world is not money; the true currency in life is trust.

TRAVELING AROUND

Throughout my career, I was very fortunate; fortunate to meet some amazing people; to work with many heroes; to work for many more heroes; to live in different countries. These experiences give me a unique perspective on the world; some of it is of course related to my personal ideology. But I feel I do possess a world view of culture rather than just one of an United States Citizen.

One of the things I learned is when you break it down, people are pretty much the same everywhere, regardless of their environment. Go into any person's home for dinner and evening and you will find that just about every family is the same. The children complain the parents are not fair. There is a drunk uncle somewhere. At some point in the evening, there will be some sort of discourse between the woman and man of the house. At another point, the men will break off, either to grill or smoke or drink or just complain and the women will do pretty much the same...only inside the dwelling. It is universal and when you think about it, it makes the world a smaller place.

The End

The Seven Things
Balance
Peace
Truth
Respect
Honour
Wisdom
Love

FEELING OLD

We are further (in years) from the release of the movie, BACK TO THE FUTURE than Marty was from 1955.

QUESTIONS

Questions; Aren't questions just lovely? You see there, that was a question about a question. My favorite questions are the ones that come from my children, *Seriously*! Now, I am a father, actually, I am a *Daddy* right now, so my view of questions from my children is very different from those of you lovely mothers out there. Daddies do not equate the barrage of questions from their children to machinegun fire faced on the beaches of Normandy or sleet against the windshield on a mountain road at mid-night as mothers do. There are a couple of reasons for this difference; one is we have developed selective hearing and often times are not listening and two; we like to have fun.

Now I realize many people think their children are brilliant and beautiful blah blah whatever. I completely understand that. I also understand no-one really cares about my children other than me so I am not going to tell you they are brilliant. There is a reason for that and it is because they are my children, which gives them a high probability of being crazy. If you ask my children what their sur-name is and then ask them what that means, they will answer, *Crazy*. True story.

Anyway, I am often amused and amazed by the questions they ask and the statements they make. When my daughter Veronica was four years old she said something along the lines of, *Daddy, I wonder what color the number three smells like*. What? That is awesome! Jesus, Mary, Joseph, what other things do you pounder little one?

Okay, for those of you with children in school here are some things to ask your kids instead of the often overused, "How was your day?"

- What were your two favorite parts of your day at school today?
- What was one challenging thing you learned today?
- What is your favorite game to play during recess?

- Tell me something that made you laugh today.
- How did you help your teacher today?
- Which three of your friends did you sit closest to during lunch?
- Did your friends bring their lunch? What did they have?
- Did your friends buy their lunch? What did they buy?
- Whom among your classmates is most / least like you?
- If you were the teacher, what would you teach your class?

OTHER RANDOM QUESTIONS

- I wonder how much deeper the ocean would be without sponges?
- Why did Kamikaze piolets wear helmets?
- If a werewolf flew a space ship and landed on the moon, would he land as a man or as a werewolf?
- Why do psychics need to ask for your name?
- Have you ever considered the reason Santa is so jolly is because he knows where all the bad girls live?
- If a cat always lands on it's feet and toast always lands with the butter side down; what would happen if you strapped a piece of buttered toast to the back of a cat and threw it out the window?
- If a tree falls in the forest and no one is around to hear it, is the husband still wrong?

THIS I BELIEVE / FAITH

A judge, I am not a judge. Your judge, I am most certainly not. Do no for one split second this I am here to judge your beliefs...I am not, nor do I care to. Neither should anybody else for that matter. The freedom of religion in the U.S.A. is so very misunderstood. It makes me wonder if anyone has actually taken the time to read the law which covers it; and I do mean anyone, citizens or politicians, Supreme Court Justices. The amendment states in part, "Congress shall make no law concerning...." That means, no law. Nothing. The feds shouldn't be saying anything about it one way or the other. Not protecting your rights or enforcing someone else's. By passing any law, anything, they are wrong. By hearing any case or lawsuit and making a ruling, they are wrong. Why is this so hard to understand? People going to the feds saying that religious displays violates my right to...blah blah, whatever... The response shoud be, "*and*?"

If it is an issue to be heard, your State government is where to go and even then, depending upon your State's Constitution, legally, you may still be told to pack sand.

Get over yourselves. Everybody; citizens, governments, courts, politicians, the whole lot. You, we, me are a tiny organism on a tiny rock floating through space. You, we, me are one of the billion of iterations life has pushed through, well, life. God has a plan for you, take it up with Him. If you don't believe in God, well, I don't know who you go take it up with, guess you are screwed.

Given all of this, my suggestion would be go find a purpose for yourself and leave the rest of us alone. If we need an external force to regulate our beliefs or show us our purpose I guarantee you governments are not it and our federal government is actually prohibited from doing so. In the grand scheme of things, you are insignificant, so am I...so what. Sew buttons. To those around you and to your family you may be important. With the right choices you may even have a happy an impactful life. Then again, perhaps not. Regardless, it is not covered by the Constitution. "…pursuit of happiness." That is all you get from the founding fathers and for all we know they could have been referring to a stripper in Philly when that was penned. If you believe in something, great. If you don't believe in something, no worries. In no law written by man is belief a requirement.

One could make the argument that restricting a person's belief is unlawful but the Constitution prohibits the federal government from passing a law which would impose such a restriction. Is any of this making any sense? If you do not like a nativity scene displayed in front of a church, no one, regardless of what they say to your face, cares. If that really offends you, what the hell are you doing at a church anyway? And why do you even recognize or acknowledge the word hell? Stop using it; it is the opposite of Heaven, which you claim not to believe in. So to hell with you. But that wouldn't make sense…um, what should I say, um, "to nowhere with you?" Ah, screw it; this has already taken up too much of my time.

To believers of all faiths, keep something in mind; you don't get to heaven on a bus or in a group, your faith is personal to you and the relationship you have with your deity. Certainly as a Christian I understand the importance of teaching my children my beliefs and there is that nugget about helping our spouses get into Heaven. Beyond that, spreading the word is about it and arguing with people is not spreading the word. You may want to stop and ask yourself why and what you are doing when engaging others about your faith or religion. (Faith and religion are two different things.) Are you taking whatever action for God's glory or for your own? For the atheists, people who believe in something does not infringe upon your, um, no beliefs. How could it, you don't believe so there is nothing of yours to offend. How can someone infringe on something you claim not to have. It would be like proving a negative. And let us be honest, most don't understand what that concept means anyway.

Now you could have skipped the previous paragraph because it has nothing to do with the fact the U.S. Government has overstepped it's authority on this issue and we the people have allowed that to happen. How about this, the next time our federal government (and it is ours, *the people*s, not the elected officials) orders something involving faith to be removed, such as the Ten Commandments from a building, simply respond you do not recognize their authority to issues such an order. Then have that pushed up the court system or watch a lower court dismiss the case entirely.

Fanatics on both sides of this issue make my brain itch and even being a practicing Catholic, give me a great argument for the use of birth control. There has been so much wickedness done in Christ's name there is no question in my mind, Christ would not do the same. As for atheists, I am surprised you do not refer to yourselves as a Non-Prophet Religion (not for profit) and apply for tax exempt status. There is no point in my directly addressing Muslims in this essay since there is no chance of an actual dialog taking place. For you Buddhists, not that you require any, but if it any consolation to you, if you are correct, I have made so many mistakes I will probably be reincarnated as myself.

Believe That

HAPPINESS

The things that make me happy may be the same things that make you happy. It wasn't always clear to me what it was in life that actually made me happy or at least I would not have been able to tell you so clearly not so long ago. So what are they, what are the things in life that make me happy? Speaking in generalities, they are things I have found which are the same for persons all over the world, regardless of culture, religion, nationality, age or race.

Things to do with personal connections.
Things to do with people
Things to do with society
Things to do with autonomy

Of course I cannot speak for everybody or anybody other than myself, but as I discovered the things in life that really brought me happiness, I was able to identify the things I want in life or more to the point, the type of life I want in my own pursuit of happiness. I want a life of meaning; a life with family; a life with of friendship; a life of intimacy; a life of sexuality; a life of sociability. These are the aspects of life which truly reflect my desires. How about you? Are you able to identify the things in life you know will bring happiness to it? If not, perhaps you should go find out.

Live

SLAVERY

I don't want to heard about big companies trading all your time and dreams for small amounts of money. I don't want to hear about outsourcing. If you see the word slavery and think about it in a metaphorical way, you are, no-offense an idiot. If you see the word and your first thought is American history, then you are too. In fact, I hope people are offended, because we all should be offended. This is not something that happened two hundred years ago and is still holding minorities back; this is happening right now! Human trafficking is real, it still exists, it is not limited to one ethnic group, and it needs more attention by everyone in the entire world. I am talking about actual slaves. The estimate as of 2018 is over forty-million people in forced labor or sexual slavery. 40 MILLION! Any rational person should suspect that the actual number is higher because I don't think slavers are really interested in reporting statistics. In the U.S.A. alone, my native country, sexual slavery was estimated as a ten-billion (with a B) dollar industry in 2017. It was reported as an industry for Christ's sake! For the love of God, I don't want to hear about anyone's ancestors when there are people in the world today being kidnapped, bred, and sold. Jesus, Mary, Joseph, why isn't this getting more attention? I will put information in the appendix where you can receive free stickers to help. These stickers, (and don't laugh jackass, this is important.), have an international toll free numbers to call if you are a victim. Place these stickers in bathroom stalls, under sinks in public restrooms, behind doors, anywhere you can think where someone who has been taken, sold, whatever may see it. Perhaps a child, someone on the ground looking up. Any place. The key is not to put it where the bad guys are looking or might see it right away. Put it somewhere where a person who is cowering, or hiding, may see it.

One-hundred-fifty-BILLION dollars a year for human traffickers according to a 2014 report from the I.L.O.. World wide, the slave trade is the second largest criminal industry. Second only behind the drug trade. The USA has a Drug Enforcement Agency; it has an Alcohol Tobacco and Firearm Agency; it has an agency for people cheating on their taxes; it even has an agency responsible for the illegal farming and selling of salmon. Where are the anti-slavery agents? Where is Interpol on this? Don't give me a bunch of crap about what we are doing either. I worked twenty-three years for the federal government under three Presidents; sat on the National Security Council; worked at the State Department; worked for the I.C. and guess what didn't get specialized attention? When was the last time you heard modern slavery brought up during any election…for any office? .Pathetic! This is the real inconvenient truth. How about our federal government stay away from my beverage straws; stop bothering me about the portion sizes of my meals; forget about putting warning labels on my music; stop changing the way children learn math; stop keeping your citizens divided with abortion and gun control every single time you need a distraction from whatever it is you are trying to get away with. I don't need to be in your thoughts and prayers. I could give a rat's ass if you are the type of person I would want to have a beer with.

Look at these countries and the numbers in modern slavery in 2017 (Again, if this is the estimate, you can bet the actual number is higher.): India, 14.3 million; China 3.2 million; Pakistan 2.1 million; North Korea 2 million (One in ten people is in a forced labor camp)

Enough Already!

JUST FOR CLARIFICATION

If you do not believe me, take my Mother L's often repeated direction and "Go look it up." If something is wrong and you know it is wrong but everyone around you thinks it is right; does that make everyone around you correct? Let me ask it another way; what would you teach your own children if they asked you? (Yeah, I know…I hit you with a gut punch. Yep. If you are a man, I caught you just below the belt and if you are a woman that is right one right to the baby maker.) This is life. There are real questions and you are all adults or you are all going to be adults one day. Sorry if nobody has mentioned that to you yet. But you don't have to always be so serious; if and when you are just remember; we're sentence here for life and none of us are getting out alive.

"*The early bird gets the worm.*" The entire thing: "*The early bird gets the worm but the second mouse gets the cheese.*"

"*Curiosity killed the cat.*" The entire thing: "*Curiosity killed the cat but satisfaction brought it back.*"

"*Rome wasn't built in a day but it burned in one.*" Some really like this because it is easy to understand and who doesn't like Italy? The great fire of Rome and Nero blah blah but I know this, no matter how hard you worked to build a reputation it can go away in an instant. Same thing for relationships don't throw away everything for a moment of pleasure small acts can wipe out years of hard work

"*jack of all tradres master of none. Though often times better than a master of one.*" Bosnians mates motto…a saliors creed.…. …

"*great minds think alike but fools rarely differ.*" So what's your point? What do you want to get across just because a mass of people agree on a situation it does not mean they have the right/correct answer.

"*blood is thicker than water*" the quote actually is "*blood of the Covenant is thicker than water of the womb*" It quote originated during times of war with the purpose of motivating soldiers to create a brotherhood that's stronger than the one formed at birth. The phrase actually means that the blood spilled during battle going through hard times together connects people in a deeper way than anything else those who are willing to die together for their common goals and values are beyond brothers

"money is the root of all evil" the actual quote is *"the love of money is the root of all evil"* Money is a tool. The actual quote about money has a subtle but very important difference in what is seen as negative that being the love of money. Paul of Taurs gets misquoted and by pushing this false agenda you are not doing anyone any favors. If you go back to the original text you will realize that the entire stance of the story is focused around sin as the source of evil with the love of money being one of the sins. Being obsessed with material things in the detriment of our values is what may lead us to having an unfilled life and regret it in the end. This is a very important difference.

"carpe diem" is an imcomplete quote. The entire quote is *"carpe diem qualm minimum credulous tarot"* which means "seize the day put very little trust in tomorrow the future" The actual meaning is more along the lines of get as many of your chores done today because maybe tomorrow you will not get a chance to and your entire life will fall apart because of your momentary neglect. Carpe diem is not a call to throwing away your future for immediate pleasures

"winning isn't everything it's the only thing." Have you noticed how losers only use the first part of this quote by Vince Lombardi? "Losers talk about how they did their best and winners go home and get to f*** the prom queen." Sean Connery in *The Rock* Up until recently, we understood this natural law. Those who have the biggest positive impact will be rewarded the most.

"birds of a feather flock together until the cat come." The second part of the quote exposes the fakeness of the reality we live in today while the first part of the quote gives way to segregation and soley based upon the same feathers. This quote is interesting to me; it outlines the idea that those who are similar in nature gravitate towards one another because they think they will be better able to relate between themselves. Which is fine until an external force, perhaps an external crippling force poses a threat to each member as an individual. When that happens, the nature of the situation changes from a group mentality to one of self-preservation. The moment that the threat reveals itself the color of your feathers no longer makes any difference and all of that nonsense will be overwritten by selfish interests. This is what I find so interesting; you can observe the exact same type of behavior even if the

opposite of the situation presents itself. The birds will fight each other for a piece of bread since personal gain oftentimes trumps the group values.

"ignorance is bliss it is folly to be wise." The phrase is from a poem by English writer Thomas Grey who was reflecting upon the notion that the more you age the more you learn about the world and the pressures of adulthood fall onto your shoulders.

"the meek shall inherit the earth" this was actually lost in translation of the word *meek* which does not mean poor or humble. The original meaning is something along the lines of *those who have the strongest weapons yet keep them shackled shall inherit the earth*

"you can't have your cake and eat it too" the actual quote is *"you can't eat the cake and still have it too"* the only problem with this quote is that the entire quote makes a lot more sense linguistically and logically than the one that is being shared around like mommy's Xanax at a slumber party. It pretty much boils down to a choice you have to make; you are either going to enjoy the cake or keep it. If you eat your cake then you no longer have it. The only reason I would ever buy a cake is because I want to eat it …so wtf?

"life is short" No it is not, so please stop talking. Actually, *Life* is the longest thing you will ever do.

Ghetto – Although the word *ghetto* is now used to identify an impoverished urban areas, this is not the original definition. The word ghetto pertained to quarters where Jewish persons were forced to live, irrespective of social class. In the early 1500s in Venice, Jews were housed on an island with an iron foundry. The Italian word for foundry is "ghèto".

UTTER NONSENSE

Just for the fun of it...

In an effort to make this book a financial pleasure, my editor Jennifer had her husband Johnny (aren't Lil' Johnny jokes funny?) suggest an order of the essays to better find my voice. So I went to an empty warehouse, whereupon shouting would produce an echo which ("ding dong the witch is dead") I followed. Inn (Joseph & Mary found no room) doing sow (reap it) I lost my shadow (me and my, with Frank [let us be] & Dean.) Of course (Pebble Beach) this meant I had to go to London (bridge is falling down) where Wendy & her brothers were learning 2 fly. After salutations Wendy, without hesitation, contemplation, deliberation, or preparation (H) promptly sewed my shadow to my boots, (..."were made for walking."). I recommenced the search for my voice. walking the line collecting `cash; Johnny Cash, "Hello I'm Johnny Cash.", he would say even though everyone knew who he was 'cause his name was on the ticket, (..."to ride, but she don't care). Then little Johnny and I went aboard, (a board more boring than boring a hole N 2 a boar), a cruise ship whereupon Sally (Mustang) fell overboard and shouted timorously which, ("Ding dong the witch is dead"), sounded caterwaul 2 me. Johnny heard her and saw sharks surrounding her as she continued yelling, "Help! Help!". Little Johnny just laughed and laughed because he knew those sharks were not going to help her. As he relished in schadenfreude, I remembered it slipped (-ery when wet) my mind (which I don't) to thank Wendy 4 sewing my shadow. Fearful she would Sioux me for basting (turkey was dry.) the shadow to my boots without pay, I fled.

POKER

The earliest memory I have playing poker was when I was in the third grade. My Father's friends taught me how to play at a kitchen table back when *crap* was a bad word and if there were ladies at the table *crud* was the strongest word I was allowed to use. My Father had a lot of good friends who were good people with nice homes and good families. My sister and I were very happy with my Father and we liked the Landmark Apartments where we lived. The only thing we didn't like was that our Daddy had to work nights, but even that was okay because on school nights we got to spend the night at a friend's house. My Father picked us up from school, helped us with our homework and then played with us. He would get ready for work as it got close to supper time, and we would all eat together at our apartment or we would all eat together at our (his) friend's house with their family. Then he would have to go to work, but he was back in the morning to get us ready and take us to school. For CAS and I, it was fun.

Learning how to play poker or any card game with your family is one thing. It's fun, lots of laughter, whole-lotta inside jokes, giggles, tickles and tones of voice. Learning how to play poker with someone else's family is another thing entirely. There was no poker for my sister and I back at our good ol' Southern Baptists Grandparent's farm we had just moved from…no siree-bobtail! But oh boy did I like cards, it was fun! There was lots of laughter and a lot of inside jokes and giggles and tickles and tones of voice there, but I was an observer. They taught me the rules and I paid attention. Everyone laughed and so did I, but I was also learning. They would giggle and I smiled and watched. They might snort while laughing and I'd laugh too but was also studying. Not even knowing what I was doing, by learning their *family* language, I was learning how to read tells.

Despite all of the kitchen table games I learned and regardless how interesting an evening of *Dealers Choice* may be, my favorite game of poker is 7 – Card Stud. "The Game of Patience", it is a slower game, but a game which does not wipe players out in the first thirty minute even though the game provides the opportunity to produce the largest pots. The popular Texas-Hold'em is just 7-Card Stud on Meth. It is popular for tournaments because the games are usually over rather quickly. But if you want to spend an evening playing cards in a game that will allow a decent player to enjoy the game for hours and will a terrific players to walk away with the most winnings, 7 – Card Stud is your answer. It is also the only game played when I am the host.

The basic rules for both 7- Card Stud and Texas Hold 'em are the same with the main differences being how often you bet, and required bets. Because I do not particularly like playing Texas Hold-'em I am not going to write much more about it. (Hey, my book, my rules…Souix me.) There was a time when the poker rooms in Vegas were pretty much an even split between these two games but in recent years it has become more difficult to find a Stud game already in progress. I always ask to start a list for a 7 – Card Stud game, and then go play Hold –'em until there are enough players on the list to being a game of 7 – Card…

"…poker is an honest profession; gambling the odds are always on the house." Val Kilmer as Doc Holiday in TOMBSTONE

Now, before this essay takes a turn towards *Boringsville* let me stop the notion anyone may have about me teaching you how to play poker. I am more than happy to school you from across the table just about any night of the week…but teaching you would be counterproductive to my potential financial pleasure and may not exactly be interesting to read for the majority of you whom I thank for purchasing my book. However, this world of ours is in dire need of, well a lot of things which mostly revolve around passion…for something. So, in an effort to create more passion or at the very least, morbid curiosity for 7-Card or poker in general, I will keep this essay light-hearted with some fact and trivial and statistics I happen to find interesting. Also, for those of you Kristin Dunce-Interview With A Vampire-"*I Want Some More*"- Hilarious-Dill Pender reference and plot point from DeadPool 2, I will direct you to a couple of excellent books for further reading. (Wow, that pop culture reference was elaborate and worth it!)

As anyone over the age of thirty-two will tell you, there are more important things in life to know besides the rules. 7-Card is no exception P' Mike my been in one of you chas

- Pay attention and remember the cards

The general rules of poker apply to 7-Card Stud (7-Card). Start with a new deck of fifty-two cards discarding (Ha!) the joker (Double Ha!) and the *rules* which come in a new pack of Bicycle Brand Cards. I bring this up, because there was an evening I found myself chasing an inside straight only to be dealt the instructions...true story; mis-deal; re-deal; I lost. What is the lesson to be learned from this? Never chase an inside straight.

If you are not certain of the rank of hands they will be in the appendix along with some information you may find useful but is not particularly interesting to read. Like the small print in an agreement with Rumpelstiltskin...not interesting, but you should know it...why? Well, (deep subject), eighty-five percent of people who play poker lose. (one-hundred percent of dogs that play poker lose regardless of what the painting depicts) Everyone thinks they know how to play poker, right? Everyone in a casino has twenty-bucks, right? So every thirty minutes or so, someone sits down at a poker table and donates twenty-bucks to the game they had no intention of staying in or actually winning. Seriously, it happens all the time and quite frankly I love it. Thank you guy in shorts with the *Yard Of Alcohol Drink* and the crumpled twenty dollar bill. You, no matter what you disapproving wife is telling you at the table, totally belong and are greatly appreciated. "Now, run along and get a shower so you can take Mrs. Personality to that show...Don't bother sobering up, she is already pissed so why bother..." quote from every soon to be divorced man in the casino.

with the largest pots... Many, many moons later, married with a baby girl, during a 7-card Stud game, in my own home, after the horse race on the first Saturday of May, a comrade divulged to the table, (Actually the entire room.), "James doesn't play cards; James plays people!" "No more Mint Juleps for you." I said while trying to recall some *probability versus gambling* nonsense I had memorized a decade, a moon, and several bourbons earlier, just to be a smart-ass while taking another's money, at such a moment. (Insert crickets making cricket noises here.) Since, of-course-I-couldn't-remember- anything, I simply smirked and folded. I am pretty certain there was more than one person in that room giving me a *tone of voice look* which said, "He teed it up for ya. Swing and a miss Johnny Moss, Bobby Jones, Ted Williams"

If you find yourself in a poker room, and are interested in a great game, ask to start a list for a game of 7-Card...if there already is a list, terrific, add your name, and if there isn't...start one...either way, I may just join you.

Check

Your *You are* Toast
The toast I gave my sister at her wedding
We have Heard The Toast For The Mother And The Daughter
We Have Toasted The Sweetheart And Wife
But Somehow We Missed Her
My Dear Little Sitter
The Joy Of Another Man's Life

BANANA REPUBLICS

"...come all the expatriated Americans..."

Making money is not that hard. Keeping the bulk of your money is. Hurray for off shore accounts! Tax havens, loopholes, whatever, the regulations are in the books and it is legal. Yep. So zip it!-Teresa-tax-taker! You and Sally-stingy-stealing-siphoning, should find a hospital, because I have no more *patients* for you. "How?" "Where ?" You ask. Grab your phone, wallet, passport, keys and I'll show you.

"...Some of them come for the sailing, drawn by the lure of the sea, to cure the spirit that's ailing, from living in the land of the free..."

Having been afforded the opportunity to live on the other side of the world for a while was a blessing, even if I did not realize it at the time. Thankfully I am a curious man with all sorts of interests. (Have you picked up on the essay's theme? afford, money, interest, [you should 'cause I'm laying it on pretty thick]) In no way shape or form am I advocating anything illegal, so relax. If I really knew how to hide money from the tax man (Great Beatles song) or a former spouse, there would still be an Aston Martin parked in my driveway. (Yeah, I had one, and I put a Harley Davidson bumper sticker on it too. Just to annoy some family members...) But there are some things I learned while living and working overseas I want to share with you. Yes, you; the person reading this, these words right now. Hi ya! Okay, what follows are some financial/business facts/regulations of some countries I just happen to know about.

"…some of them are running from lovers, leaving no forward address. Some of them are running marijuana and some are running from the IRS…"

Let us start with a country everyone, anyone, all of us, knows about even if we don't know how we know it. Switzerland. Switzerland has the most stable banking sector in the world.

The United Arab Emerites (UAE) is the offshore financial center of the Arabian Gulf. (FYI, Arabs do not like or refer to the region as the Persian Gulf, to them it is the Arabian Gulf. Since they had their special forces fighting beside our special forces, on this point, I respect their wishes.) Dubai is to New York as Abu Dhabi is to Washington DC. Yes, there are luxurious residences and hotels. But the cities remind me of Las Vegas. There is much glamour and lights and fun, just don't look behind the curtain for the wizard unless you are prepared to see the disenfranchise work. The UAE is a tax haven and establishing a company in any of the many free trade zones could not be simpler. If you and your money are looking for a place to call home, it is very easy to start a new life there.

"…late at night you can see them, in the cheap hotels and bars.
Hustling the senoritas as they dance beneath the stars…"

Another option in the region is Bahrain. The island of oil and gas is also a discrete financial deposit point. Although many people disagree with me (shocking…not) I would not recommend starting a business there because it is very expensive and it will take you some time, (a month or so) to establish. But if you have the means, I do know of two people who told me it is worth it.

"…learn the native customs, a word of Spanish or two. Then you know
you can't trust them because they know they can't trust you…"

Cayman Islands has no corporate tax and by some measures is the world's sixth largest banking center. *

Luxemburg is one of the oldest tax havens in existence. Offshore bank accounts are tax exempt as are long term capital gains are paid on stocks.

For one-hundred-bucks, I bet you aren't expecting the next place I write about. Do you take that bet? You do! Deal!!! Cool. Germany. Yep. Germany. (It's okay, you can owe me.) In Germany incorporated offshore companies needn't disclose beneficial owners. There is no way to be certain how long that policy will be in place. The European Union (EU) is having a time right now with the U.K. exiting the EU. But for now it is an option.

Hong Kong has autonomy being the first special administrative region of China. Individual wealth in Hong Kong is among the highest per capita in the world. It has a substantial fund management industry and billions in private banking assets.

Lebanon has extremely strict bank secrecy regulations. Their own Ministry of Finance has no access to money transaction information or banking customers identity within the financial sector. Furthermore, offshore companies there are tax exempt. Plus, they love to grill their steaks and other dead animals and they appreciate women who like to dance...for men... while they eat charred dead animals...Seriously, I love it there. It is like Texas without tornados...

Singapore has no tax on earnings under two million dollars. That and cheap beer will satisfy any trust-fund-million-dollar-baby.

United States of America... While causing a raucous over foreign tax havens, the USA is a business tax haven itself. Arizona, Delaware, Montana, Navada, New York, Wyoming are home to a great many ghost companies and no one seems to notice or care about it. If you don't get involved in politics you may be left alone. If you decide to get involved inpolitics just remember to donate big, both ways. Every multi-billionaire has and does and one of them ended up......To be continued..............

CONSIDER THE SOURCE

Five Major Corporations:
The New York Times Company owns the Boston Globe
The Washington Post owns NewsWeek
Disney owns ABC
CBS owns Simon & Schuster
Time Warner owns CNN, AOL, Time, Warner Bros. Studio, HBO, New Line Cinema, Sports Illustrated, People, Fortune, Money
News Corporation owns the Wall Street Journal, Fox Television, London's The Times, Barron's, Harper Collins, Hulu, Zondervan, The New York Post

HISTORY

The thing to keep in mind about history is it repeats itself. The thing to keep in mind about history is it repeats itself. The thing to keep in mind about history is it repeats itself. The thing to keep in mind about history is it repeats itself. The thing to keep in mind about history is it repeats itself. The thing to keep in mind about history is it repeats itself. The thing to keep in mind about history is it repeats itself. The thing to keep in mind about history is it repeats itself. The thing to keep in mind about history is it repeats itself. The thing to keep in mind about history is it repeats itself. The thing to keep in mind about history is it repeats itself. The thing to keep in mind about history is it repeats itself. The thing to keep in mind about history is it repeats itself. The thing to keep in mind about history is it repeats itself. The thing to keep in mind about history is it repeats itself. The thing to keep in mind about history is it repeats itself. The thing to keep in mind about history is it repeats itself. In the simplest of definitions, history seems not to have started until man began to record significant actions. History did not begin to make sense until women began to edit what man had documented. The thing to keep in mind about history is it repeats itself. The thing to keep in mind about history is it repeats itself. The thing to keep in mind about history is it repeats itself. The thing to keep in mind about history is it repeats itself. The thing to keep in mind about history is it repeats itself. The thing to keep in mind about history is it repeats itself. The thing to keep in mind about history is it repeats itself. The thing to keep in mind about history is it repeats itself. For the meaning of life turn to last page of this book. The thing to keep in mind about history is it repeats itself. The thing to keep in mind about history is it repeats itself. The thing to keep in mind about history is it repeats itself. The thing to keep in mind about history is it repeats itself. The thing to keep in mind about history is it repeats itself. The thing to keep in mind about history is it repeats itself. The thing to keep in mind about history is it repeats itself. The thing to keep in mind about history is it repeats itself.

VENI, VIDI, VICI

Perhaps the most concise after action report in history. Not at all surprising when you realize Julius Caesar was a warrior just as hostel soldier before he was a politician. Interesting fact about persons of action; military, LEO, agent, case officers, merc, any of the people who would rather spend their time in the field and nowhere near the flag pole, they despise paperwork and hate writing reports. This is a constant problem. The reason it is a problem is, generally speaking, for every hour of fun you have in the field, (yes, field work can be fun...a lot of fun), there is at a minimum two hours of reporting requirements. Okay, maybe that is a slight exaggeration, but in today's world, not by much. If you were to place a pen and a pistol in front of any of these professionals and give them a choice between writing a report or shooting themselves...they would all pause to think about it.

After action reports, Reports Of Investigation, whatever they are called are not exactly fun to write. Caesar had it right.

I'll Write The Rest Of This Later

FYI

The *FED,* has nothing more to do with the U.S. Federal Government than Federal Express…and the Chairman whom sets interests rates has absolutely nothing to do with the Department of Treasury…

Just think about that…and then go read some history as to hoe and why we got here…(I'll give you a starting point…research a prominent war hero, lawyer, diplomat, born in the islands and killed in a duel…(I've said too much…)

SANTA CLAUSE

Perhaps Santa is so jolly because he knows where all the bad girls live.

Yes, Santa is real, I responded when my daughter Maria asked me. This question did not cause me to fall into daddy-panic-mode. Without pausing to think I knew it was up to me to ensure she continued to find credence in the magically wonderful aspects of living in a less than magically wonderful world. Santa is real. If my oldest was asking me now, her siblings would be asking her soon. If she believed, the idea would gain traction with her sister and brother. I wasn't worried about doing my part right so this would be the only time I had to answer this question. Is Santa real? Okay.

At that point my daughter was working on the supposition Santa exists and is real. There was evidence beyond the presents. There was the Elf on the Shelf. (Do you do that is your home? What did your children name their elf? My children named their efl *Dillon*...my children are weird.) We put out milk and cookies on Christmas Eve with a note. The cookies and milk are consumed and the note has a reply. We draw huge "welcome" and "stop here" signs with chalk in the street and drive way on Christmas Eve. These little family traditions are something we all enjoy allowing us to become involved in an event instead of just witnessing one. These are things I am prepared to do and look forward to doing for as long as there are others to do them with.

When my daughter asked me, I simply said yes and that was that. Ah, I miss those days...the days when my child would ask me a question and a simple one word answer was all that was required. No need to explain the validity of my CVs. No follow up questions, no "if it pleases the court." Question and answer.

Santa is real. How do I know, how can I prove it? Well, (deep subject), in my own home with my own family, I have attributed gifts to my children as being from Santa. On the same Christmas mornings, I have received gifts from Santa. So obviously I am not Santa even when I acted as Santa. So, someone must be Santa. There you go, as clear as a glass of muddy water. Is Santa real because we are all Santa to each other? Okay.

Yes, I have been to the North Pole. There is a piece of property and a house said to be Santa's. I didn't see Santa, or elves, or a workshop. There were reindeer, but I didn't see them fly. If you mail a letter to Santa through the U.S. Postal Service it goes somewhere. As a child I wanted to know where and if got to Santa. So, thinking I was clever, I wanted to send a letter to Santa return-receipt. My step-dad obliged the ever so inquisitive nature of a ten year old boy. Guess what, I got a return signed by Santa. Who signed it? It said Santa.

Belief Acceptance Faith Trust View Ideology Credence Feeling Confidence Reliance Conviction Is Santa a state of mind? Okay.

One of my favorite* Christmas songs is "I Believe" by Frank Sinatra.

"…and when it's Christmas I believe in Santa Clause. Why do I believe, I guess I believe because…"

I believe because I choose to believe.

*My favorite Christmas song is "A Patrick Swayze Christmas"

MURDER BY NUMBERS

Kinda like *Death By Power Point* a phrase any person employed by the Federal Government after Mr. Gates provided his operating system for free to the government…(Is it just me, or are power point presentations the worst thing to site through…other than Pre Kana, and any funeral, and most movies on the Halmark Channel)

- 363 Pilgrams killed over one weekend in Mecca in a stampede at the annual hajj. The event easily brings over three million people to the city.
- 2,500 number of persons trampled to death at the event from 1990 to 2004

The Theatre

- 7,486 was the number of performances Phantom of the Opera needed to overtake CATS as the longest running Broadway in history.
- 120 million people have attended Phanton of the Opera since it opened in 1988

Land use in CONUS (Contiental United States) as of May 2019 according to USDS, Dept. of the Interior, BLM, Forest Service

- 654 million acres of pastures
- 538 million acres of forests
- 391 million acres of farmland/crops
- 69 million acres of urbanized areas

The next number is interesting to me; not because of the number itself, but the different uses of land the government chose to group together when reporting this number.

- 168.7 million acres of defensive facilities, airports, golf courses, and parks in the United States.

BATMAN

(Superman too)

In my previous book an essay about which actor I considered thought was the best representation of James Bond, as described in the original Ian Fleming novels received the most e-mail responses. This is a book which contained essays on immigration, same sex marriage, hate crimes, the pope, as well as jokes, quotes, clichés and Frank Sinatra among other topics. It was interesting to me which essay provoked readers the most. A statement I made about BATMAN being the greatest superhero did result in a few messages most of which asked whom I considered the best BATMAN and why I didn't mention it. Over the years I have learned you cannot please all of the people all of the time; and most of those people were at my divorce mediation...

So, without requiring you to read multiple paragraphs about Batman I will jump right in this second paragraph and declare the following: Probably because of my age and the fact the movie came out when I was in high school and I took a hot date on opening night, Michael Keaton in the 1989 film Batman was and is the best Batman to me. Hold on now, this will get worse for some of you.

As far as the best portrayal of Bruce Wayne, I vote Ben Affleck in Batman v Superman, seriously. In the following film Suicide Squad he was only shown as Batman and carried the same darkness as before, but Bruce Wayne was absent from that film. Unfortunately in the movie JUSTICE LEAGUE, his characters, Bruce Wayne and Batman were basically reduced to comic relief; completely abandoning the brutal, cynical, bitter attitude and disappointment of a man who has spent more than half of his life being let down by humanity. Keaton played Batman straight and with a slightly comedic Wayne possessing a solitary alter ego. There are deleted scenes of Val Kilmer reaching for the different aspect of Bruce Wayne's personality, but unfortunately they did not make it into the released film. Keaton and Christian Bale also commented on the different aspects of Bruce Wayne himself, but I think Affleck displayed it best. He played four characters in BATMAN v SUPERMAN; First as Batman, using the batsuit not so much as a mask but a uniform. Second as Bruce Wayne as a mask/disguise in a media filled/covered public social event where he was expected to be a certain person. Then as Bruce Wayne as a detective/undercover/playboy in the fightclub and finally, Bruce Wayne as he is while alone with Alfred in his residence and in the Batcave.

Now, let me blow your mind with my final entry…wait for it…the best overall portrayal of Batman/Bruce Wayne I have seen in a movie is Lego Batman in the LEGO BATMAN MOVIE. You have followed me this far down the rabbit hole, so don't give up on me now. In the Lego movie, every incarnation of Batman is referenced and incorporated into the character. The movie actually has him wearing his cowl in most of his daily life while removing it displays his "mask" Bruce Wayne. From the solitude of his microwave dinners, to his personal adrenal-pumping music playlist the movie certainly showed a diverse character.

Okay now, I mentioned Superman in the title for my cousin Scott and my adopted niece Shalyan. It is not your fault. Superman is a hard story to tell. As an introspective character instead of the world's most positive, happy, heroic, perfectly together Boy Scout, it doesn't work. Seriously, what can anyone really do with a character that is basically an all-powerful god unless he comes into contact with kryptonite which turns him into a virgin on prom night, a day late to the prom. His struggles are just something us Earthlings cannot relate to.

That's Enough

A List of Twenty

1. Avoiding Change
2. Acting Without Contemplatation
3. Being Impatient
4. Being Misunderstood
5. Believing You Are Owed
6. Blaming Yourself For What Is Out Of Your Control
7. Dwelling On Past Decisions
8. Failing Without An Attempt
9. Feeling Sorry For Yourself
10. Focusing On Weakness
11. Giving Into Fears
12. Having A Closed Mind
13. Jealously Over The Success Of Others
14. Letting Others Make Decisions For You
15. Not Listening To Advice From Others
16. Not Accepting Help
17. Repeating Mistakes
18. Staying In Your Comfort Zone
19. Trying To Please Everyone
20. Missing The Point

ARE ANGELS REAL

My daughter asked this question of me. "Are Angels real?" How do you answer such a direct and simple question from your child? Easily of course; I responded that I believed they were real but that was not her question. She didn't ask my opinion or what I believed, she asked a direct question. So I told her directly that Angels are real and I know this to be true because she is an Angel. There are few moments in life as special as the first time you see your darling sweet child roll her eyes at you. They grow up so fast.

Now that I have shared that touching moment with you perhaps you might enjoy reading some more…not about my precocious child, but about Angels.

The word Angel is based on the Hebrew word malak, which means, "messenger". Nowadays, the word angel has many more meaning, depending upon the language, culture, even dialect. A two hour search of the internet, (that is the usual amount of time it takes to look something up on the internet vs looking something up in an encyclopedia), will have results ranging from a baseball team, a musical band, some adult sites, entertainment companies and other businesses. Apparently, Angels are in vogue in the secular world.

Those who know me know I love books and if you took a gamble on me having books on this subject, well played. Just about all of the books on the subject in my home, except the encyclopedias, are faith or religious based books. (As I have written in another essay, I separate faith and religion; to me faith is created by God and religion is created by man.) So our books, while interesting and even enlightening are only from one point of view. Oh well, to quote Bugs Bunny, "*Sioux me.*"

- The Catechism states, "the existence of the spiritual, non-corporeal beings the Bible and scripture call Angels a truth of faith." Pretty direct, if you believe.
- The Old Testament mentions Angels and/or God's messengers just over one-hundred times if you count them both.
- The New Testament mentions Angels one-hundred-sixty times.
- Angels are a common aspect of many other religions and faith traditions.
- Many Non- Judeo-Christian religions have specific prayers to Angels asking for interventions or protection.
- According to tradition, there are nine *Orders* or *Choirs* of Angels:

1. Seraphim
2. Cherubim
3. Thrones
4. Dominations/Dominions
5. Virtues
6. Powers
7. Principalities
8. Archangels
9. Angels

Finally, I consider my children to be Angels from God; messengers who makes me better person and bring me joy.

I have always like to consider a group of bikers wearing helments angles.. Not Hell's Angel's, but angels. I like the think the same of certain truckers… So God Bless Bikers and Truckers.

Amen

RULES

Animals live and exist in natural cycles, (except for the ones which we have altered for our own uses and, shocking, we have screwed up…mad cow disease anyone.), and you never hear them complain and do you want to know why, because they cannot talk! (That reminds me of a joke my daughter once told me; *Daddy, why can't the dinasaurs talk? BECAUSE THEY ARE ALL DEAD!)* Humans seem to love rules and regulations. There are three agencies responsible for the farming, stability, and harvesting of salmon; a species of fish which naturally, on their own, travel thousands of miles in a lifetime finding their way back to their hometown(river) just to get it on with the one that got away from their youth. Not only do they possess a nostalgic ticket to bone-town, (which should be the envy of any ten-year-high-school-reunion), they do it without a GPS or Facebook.

Rules of the jungle; Who's lying? Speaking of lions; wow…the females hunt for food, care for the cubs and let the males sleep all day, eat, have sex, and only keep one around the pride. Oh, and the males are called King, but enough about medieval Europe…

In many ways I feel the many rules of society has inadvertently developed a prison for us. Laws, rules, regulations, dogma all created by man. God did not imprison us, we did. If you believe in Jewish history as I do, God only gave us ten rues and if you find any logic in George Carlin's humor those ten can be broken down into three, because many are repetitive. Regardless, if you start with God's set of ten, look at how many we have now…laws that is. The state of Florida just passed a law stating it is illegal to text while driving and you can be pulled over and fined. Okay, but how is it not illegal to write a letter with a pen and paper while driving? So, the state's *safety* argument is a crock. It simply gives law enforcement another articulable fact for probable cause to pull you over…and to possibly create more income for the state. Now listen, I was law enforcement, so do not think for a second I am speaking ill about LEOS, because I am not. Quite frankly, when I was a uniformed officer I would have loved to have another articulable fact to stop a bad guy. But for crying out loud, the state is not even trying to hide it anymore.

1997 U.S. Border Patrol Written Entrance Exam For Class 334

This should bring back some memories to my fellow BP Agents out there. (Those agents whom passed their 10 month.) Okay, so this isn't how the Federal Government actually ended up with such outstanding agents such as myself; but based upon the opinion of some of those we encountered, it could have been. This was back in the 90's when the U.S. Border patrol was still part of DoJ/INS and is based on those annoying e-mails we all used to forward to each other, filling up other people's in-boxes before we could fill up FaceBook pages. Enjoy.

ENTRANCE EXAM FOR THE U.S. BORDER PATROL
(This is not the Actual Exam…it's a joke)
Time Limit: 3 WEEKS

1. What language is spoken in France?
2. Give a dissertation on the ancient Babylonian Empire with particular reference to architecture, literature, law and social conditions OR-Give the first name of John Hancock.
3. Would you ask William Shakespeare to: _____ (a) build a bridge, _____ (b) sail the ocean, _____ (c) lead an army or _____ (d) WRITE A PLAY
4. What religion is the Pope? (check only one) _____ (a) Jewish_____ (b) Catholic
5. Metric conversion. How many feet is 0.0 meters?
6. What time is it when the big hand is on the 12 and the little hand is on the 5?
7. How many commandments was Moses given? (Approximately)
8. Six kings of England have been called George, the last one being George the Sixth. Name one other.
9. Can you explain Einstein's Theory of Relativity? _____ (a) yes _____ (b) no

10. An illegal alien carrying 50lbs of cocaine runs past you and steals a car while kidnapping a 3 year old child, what do you do? (a) sit there (b) write an intel report when you get back to the station (c) finish the comics and call relief to get a burger

11. Which of the following best describes your ability to perform the rigorous duties of a Border Patrol Agent. (Choose only one!)

(A) I have the ability to sleep sitting up with my head tilted back to insure that the drool slides down my throat.

(B) I have the uncanny ability to ignore all stupid request thrown at me by management without needing the assistance of the EAP.

(C) I can drive around for 10 solid hours and get absolutely NOTHING accomplished.

(D) If actually required to accomplish SOMETHING I am confident that I will be able to get "it" accomplished with the least amount of effort on my part.

OR (E) I am really good at driving drunk!

HAPPINESS

The laughter of my children is awesome and infectious. They are young therefore not self-conscious, (although Maria is almost there). They are young so stifling a giggle or a belly laugh or hiding any emotion isn't part of the program right now. They are young, so mastering the task of blowing noses or swallowing saliva before: laughing, sneezing, blowing out birthday candles, talking, singing, eating, crying, hell sleeping, has never crossed their impossibly huge brains. (I guessing here based upon the size of their heads in relation to their bodies; My children are not 'orange on a toothpick' big like "Head" in...come on, name the movie...but I want to dress them up like bobble-heads for Halloween before they level out.). So when my children laugh, it is usually an event which includes bodily fluid. Which sounds gross, because it is! Also, I have two young daughters which means if the laughing is too intense, urine and a *change of clothes will be involved as well. But, none of that matters to me at all when I hear them and watch them react to things they think are funny, especially when it is all three of them. (When it is just one-on-one, whomever is with me is normally cracking me up.) It is like eating crap amusement park or carnival food for me; I know I will deal with the repercussions for ingesting it, but the present is so enjoyable I simply do not care.

THANKSGIVING

Holidays with family, what special times they are. What is your favorite holiday to spend with your friends and family? Time with loved ones is important and special. As with many people I know, Thanksgiving ranks right up there with Christmas and Easter as a favorite time of year. But I will take it one step further and make the argument Thanksgiving many be the best holiday to spend with family, especially extended family. Let's see, since there are no gift requirements, it is cheaper than Christmas. Taking place over a four day weekend it is shorter than Easter Break and the combined Christmas and New Year's holiday. Plus you are legitimately able to excuse yourself for arriving late and departing early because, you know, *gotta travel, can't take the children out of school*, yadda yadda. Plus, there is just as much booze consumed, perhaps only second to New Year's Eve. Even with all of that being said, let's talk about what is being said. There are the things you can get away with saying over the entire Thanksgiving weekend which are socially unacceptable to utter at most any other gathering. You have probably heard some these over the years, or at least some variation of them. But I, like other members in my family, have a way with, um, communicating, so I have come up with some more *offensive-but-plausibly-explainable* things to say, ask and talk about. Therefore, in an effort to make your next Turkey Day more enjoyable as you sit with people you love but may not particularly like, I have created a list. Below are some tried and truly borderline subjects, statements and questions to make Thanksgiving dinner more interesting. Bonus points if you and your Favorite Uncle and Cousins clandestinely machinate to use the entire list in one day.

Before Dinner Subjects

- People
- Breasts
- Legs
- Race and Culture
- You'll know it's ready when it pops up.
- How long do I beat it before it's ready?

Before Dinner Questions & Statements

- How many people can you handle at a time?
- How many people have you had in the past?
- Do you think everyone will come?
- Bet you didn't expect everyone to come at once.
- I usually just spread open the legs and stuff it in.
- How long will it take after you stick it in?

During Dinner

- Ask the youngest children what they learned about Thanksgiving in school and then continually ask people if they like Indian Food.
- That's the biggest one I've ever seen. (Is this this biggest one you have ever seen?)
- When I was younger I could just keep going but now, give me a little time and I will be ready to go again.
- Tying the legs together keeps the inside moist.
- Don't have the opportunity at home, so I'm in the mood for some dark meat.
- It's a little dry, do you still want to eat it?
- Just wait your turn, you'll get some.

After Dinner

- Talk about a huge breasts!
- If I don't undo my pants, I'll burst

- Whew, that was one terrific spread
- You still have a little bit on your chin.
- Wow, I didn't think I could handle all of that
- Grab this, pull and make a wish

FRANK SINATRA

- He would practice his breathing by holding his breath underwater in his pool. As a life long smoker, he felt it was necessary.
- He always played his solo sets straight, only joking while onstage with his crew. (Unlike Dean Martin often refrain, *If you want to hear me sing seriously, buy an album.*)
- He was a real human being with real problems.
- In his younger MGM years, he rarely slept, relying mostly on catnaps.
- He doted on his children.
- He doted on broads.
- He painted.
- His favorite color was orange.
- One of his best movie roles was in the movie *SUDDENLY.*
- He should have have an OSCAR for his role in *The Man With Golden Arm*
- He insisted Elvis wear a tuxedo when the appeared together on his television show upon Elvis' being discharged from the Army.
- Some people considered him a bully
- Some people considered him a hero of the *little guy*
- He had more comebacks than herpes.
- He smoked, he drank, he loved, he fought, he won, he lost, was happy and sad…he lived a life.

EDGAR ALLAN POE

Known for his *POE-try,*
A joke which cannot be credited to me
No matter how I wish it to be
E.A.P.

The idol; The man; The legend; The myth; The poet; The person.

It is humbling for me to consider that by the time Edgar Allan Poe was my age, he ad already been dead four years. All of the things we, melancholy-misunderstood-white-privilaged-tourchered-souls-aspireing-authors want to be while we tell tail(s) heart(felt). Why do so many writers dream a dream within a dream about E.A.P. when we should realize we will never be able to reach his level any more than the conquistadors found gold in El Dorado. Face it, E.A.P. had it all as far as being an inspired artists went. I mean everything; terrible parents, awful health; poverty; alcoholism; death of his wife; nine-tine nervous breakdowns; and his own death under less than natural causes…and accomplished all this before the age of forty-two. Yeah, I know, he didn't make it into the twenty-nine club, but still. We should all accept the fact that some people are just born into it while others have to work towards it.

Interesting fact about many of Mr. Poe's poems I discovered in the seventh grade attending Crestview Junior High School; you can read *The Raven* to the tune of the *Battle Hym of The Republic.* But I must warn you, as I warned my classmates many moons ago; if you do this once, you may always do it, every time, for the rest of your life…whether you want to or not. Okay, alright, you have been warned.

PERFECT HARMONY

"I'd like to teach the world to sing, in perfect harmony..." Who remembers that particular Coca-Cola Commercia? If you do, you just 'dated' yourself, because it is from the 1970s with a slight reboot in the 1990s. Before I continue, who remembers the entire McDonalds Big Mac jingle? "Two all-beef patties, special sauce, lettuce, cheese, pickles, onion on a sesame seed bun.." You are busted. Too old to lust after NFL cheerleaders (college cheerleaders were out of reach eons ago you pervert) and the age where no handsome woman can sing "I Love Rock N Roll" without sounding creepy.

One world government. The only way I can envision I this without a dystopia would be after an alien invasion. Otherwise you have the prior mentioned dystopia or all the worst parts of the Bible describing the End of Days. To exist, it would have to be a world that accepted everyone's beliefs or outlawed all beliefs. The latter is more realistic. What about language? There would have to be one worldwide accepted language. And not the mesh-mash system used in many of the world's economic cities of today. Places where the language of business is *A* and the local language is *B* and the understood slang language is *C*. From my experience, you can survive almost anywhere without understanding the local language however you will never understand the local culture if you do not understand the language. This brings us to, *no more local culture*. It would be about as entertaining as a Arab strip-tease; think of every strip-mall in every suburb in the U.S.A.. Every parking lot has a two franchise restaurants and after a while every dinner blows.

It is our differences that make us interesting to one another. There are aspects of other cultures I enjoy and others of that same culture which make me glad they are not a part of mine. This is okay, really it is. You can appreciate and begrudge at the same time. It is called being human. Nothing is perfect in this world of ours nor should we try to make it. First of all, because we cannot, we wouldn't know where to start or where to end. Sometimes I dream about what a perfect life would be like...and I simply cannot do it, it doesn't last. Without some sort of trial or challenge or conflict or disappointment nothing would be special. If I were able to run the pool table every time someone said "rack-em", who would play me? In my younger years, if every girl I walked up to said yes to a dance, or immediately gave me her number or agreed to go out with me would I ever remember any of them? Who would be special or more important, who would be special to me. Sometimes it is the failure and the rejection that makes us put in more effort or try harder or simply change and grow...or grow up.

"Hold it! Hold it!" This is not to say I enjoy failing...I hate it, which is why I am thankful it doesn't happen that often...I jest, (but not really), of course I do, (not often), just an average guy, (with above average stats), a regular John, (who's name is James), who just happens to know what a *John* is...it's a toilet. Geesh, enough with the hooker jokes. I'm just an average Joe with all the short comings, (opinions vary), as anyone else, (who is awesome), only with a touch, (the bucket fell on me), of confidence, (sounds better than arrogance), God bestowed on me, (thank you Lord), for which I am thankful, (and some of you are grateful).

One world government...a new world order...no thank you. I'll deal with the bad just to enjoy the good. It is worth the risk to me. ...I'll put fifty on 0/00 and probably chase it for a while. It certainly makes an evening memorable and a memory a story.

That's Enough For Now.

IT'S A DIFFERENT WORLD - GET A LIFE

- It is a different world from when we were younger; your child's babysitter has seven body piercings and none are visible.
- It is a different world; you make over $100,000 and it makes financial sense to rent rather than own a house (in many cities).
- It is a different world; you take a bus and are shocked at two people carrying on a conversation in English.
- Get a life if you take the bus to listen to other people's conversation.
- It is a different world; a cup of coffee in a drive thru costs the same as a beer in a bar.
- Get a life if you have a very strong opinion about where your coffee beans are grown and tell people you can taste the difference between Sumatran and Ethiopian.
- Get a life if you know which restaurant serves the freshest arugula.
- It is a different world; your hairdresser is straight; your plumber is gay; your Mary Kay rep is a guy in drag.
- It is a different world; you pass an elementary school playground and the children are all busy with their smart phones
- Get a life if you are constantly passing elementary school playgrounds to watch the children…it's creepy

47TH BIRTHDAY

My children love to ask about the things I did as a kid, or when I was their age.. This is for them and for my friends…We laugh at things because they are funny and we laugh at things because they are true.

When I got home from school, I ate raw cookie dough from a plastic sleeve while watching cartoons, then I did my homework, while watching General Hospital so I was able to converse with the girls on the bus, then played Atari 2600 until I had to go to the bathroom, then went outside to play until the street lights came on. (There was no way to pause Asteroids or Defender, so if you had to get up, the game was over…and if you accidently moved the ship in Asteroids, the game was also over.) "Scooby Doo."was what I watched… Daphne was hot, long brfore Jessica Rabbit, *"I'm not bod; Im just drawn that way."* We had no idea Shaggy was smoking something in the back of the mystery machine, which is why he was so hungry all the time. Oh, side note, I hated Scrappy. On weekends I would sleep over at friends' houses, (the home life at my mother's wasn't pleasant.) We played army with G.I. Joe figures, and set up galactic wars between the Autobots and GoBots and green army men and Legos. (There was nevera battle, just the setting up) Not one person do I know of my amongst my friends ever solved a Rubik's cube without taking off the stickers. The Rubik's Pyramid was a joke. At six a.m., on Saturday mornings I got up watch "violent "Hanna-Barbera cartoons, such as, "The Snorks," "Jabber-jaw," "Captain Caveman," "Space Ghost," and "Super-friends." In between I would watch "School House Rock." (*"Conjunction junction, what's your function?!"*) My Dad laughed at Loony Toons more than I did; now I watch those same Loony Toons with my own children and laugh more than they do…so *Sioux me*. On Friday Night Daisy Duke was gonna be my girlfriend; her or Wilma from Buck Rodgers. I was going to own the General Lee and shoot dynamite arrows out the back and if I wrecked the car jumping over a creek it would all be okay, because Michael Knightt was going to ask me to be his replacement and KITT knew who I was. Did anyone else's Dad or Step-Dad turn from a mild-mannered wandering doctor into "The Incredible Hulk" when he got upset? I wasn't allowed to watch Revenge of Nerds when my family got the sliding-controlled cable box, but I was able to piece together the movie and how the Nerds beat the AlphaBetas over several months of peeking through the house plants behind the china cabinet at the end of the hall. I never got caught, but looking back, I am pretty certain my parents knew I was there. Sunday School teachers tried to make the Gospels interesting by not caring about the difference between the Old and the New Testaments and telling us to watch Indiana Jones save the Ark of the Covenant. It didn't make me curious about Jesus or Faith, but I was definitely going to learn how to use a bull whip, wear a hat and not shave. I had no idea what Yoda meant when he said, "No, there is another." Everyone thought President Ronald Reagan was cool when he got shot and walked into the hospital. Gorbachev was the guy with a birthmark on his forehead and who let Russian children finally have a Happy Meal by letting McDonalds open in Moscow. I collected Star Wars Movie glasses and The Muppet Movie glasses from either Burger King or McDonalds. I made certain we got a Miami Dolphin glass from the gas station when my parents filled up the car. (Between those glasses and the plastic cups I never sold from my youth soccer and football teams, our family had more than enough vessels to serve beverages to all four children through grade school, high school and college...They gave me a set of eight Mobile Gas Station Miami Dolphin glasses when I rented my first apartment without a co-signer and without a roommate.) I listened to John *Cougar* Mellencamp and couldn't wait to put my hand between Diane's knees. Boy George was the most popular girl's Halloween costume in the fourth grade at Most Holy Redeemer Catholic Grade School and we all wondered why his dreams were, *red, gold and green*. Duran Duran did a James Bond Theme, Friday Night Videos was a popular show, "You can't Do That On Television" was awesome and who else remembers Danger-mouse? Yes, I was happy we still had HBO when Mike Tyson beat Michael Spinks in under thirty-seconds. PayPerView Fights were not a thing then but if they were I am pretty certain my parents would have told me it was a waste of money. The cool white guy from WKRP In Cincinnati was Mike Tyson's wife's teacher in Head of the Class. I was too young to care about or try TAB, but I knew Shasta was what we bought for neighborhood block parties. We had Charlie's Chips delivered once a month buy a cargo truck in a big tan tin can. My sister and I got in trouble every month for eating the entire can in less than two weeks. Capri Sun was a pain to drink, but I still wanted it in my metal Empire Strikes Back lunch box. The lunch box thermos was all of a sudden filled with wasted tomato soup. We traded Little Debbie Snack Cakes at the lunch table. "Move Over Bacon, There Is Something Leaner" is a phrase I still say, because as I remember it, Sizziline was awesome! The school science fair was always rigged and my parents helped us less and less each passing year. Field day was as anticipated as much as the last day of school but it always rained. (This hasn't changed; No joke, this year during my children's filed day…yep, it rained…I laughed.) I bought Star Wars figures at Zayers for four dollars each. Albertson's grocery store had a toy isle that rivaled Lionel Playworld. Lionel Playworld was the best until, "*I don't wanna grow up but if I did; I'd still be a Toys R Us kid!*" We sang "*Deck the Halls with Gasoline, fala la la la, la la la la,*" and didn't get in trouble. Rubber band fights were cool and some parents even bought their children real rubber-band-firing-guns. Walking into the classroom and seeing the movie projector set up was like Christmas. A substitute teacher was either really cool or never seemed to come back. The Challenger exploded. Half of everyone's parents got divorced. There were a lot of *very special episodes* on TV. I wore the house key around my neck. My little brother wore the house key around his neck using the chain from my Father's dog-tags from Vietnam for one day. (My Father wore that dog-tag chain through the war, getting shot, earning a Purple Heart and awarded a Bronze Star; my little brother broke that chain on the his first day of high school.) We were not allowed to answer the phone if no adult was in the house but if we did, we were not to tell anyone our parents were not home. Friday nights meant going to the grocery store to rent a movie to watch. (Does anyone else remember renting a VCR for the night from the grocery store too?) The news covered AIDS but didn't cover the boy in our grade school who died of Leukemia. The local news mentioned Chrissy Schaffer from our high school who was killed on a ride at the carnival, but if you blinked you missed it. We all knew at least one person from our school who died before graduation. *Just Say No* was a joke. At least one of our Grandparents died from cancer. I played with Bristol Blocks, kept my Legos in my parent's left over frozen margarita buckets. When our parents were bowling, we played video games in the arcade with quarters carried in a purple velvet Crown Royal bag. I had a Bat Machine Big Wheel (which was the Green Machine only blue with Batman stickers and it was awesome!) Getting a bike for Christmas was the biggest and greatest gift ever! (I remember all five bikes I received in my childhood at Christmas.*) I put baseball cards in the spokes of my bike until I learned coke cans made a louder noise…but they eventually cut your tires. My sister's had streamers on their handle bars, I had *donuts* on my grips. Everyone in the family seemed to have their own style of bicycle: my step-dad had a beach cruiser, mother had the same lame big seat bike as Nana; my sisters had ten-speeds and after my Schwinn I had a BMX. I shot green army men with my BB gun in the back yard and never got in trouble for it. I did get in trouble for digging a hole in the back yard with the army surplus folding shovel. (Apparently the strategic value of foxholes for water-baloon-fights was lost upon adults.) Everyone in the family had a job to do when it was time to mow the yard; until I was big enough to push the lawn mower…then it was all me. The entire neighbor was our backyard. We used a skin board on the grass of the mean neighbor when it rained and when playing football, two pass completions was a first down, in pick-up tackle football games we played in the street. I don't remember anyone getting hurt and all arguments were settled with a *do-over*. We ran races from one mailbox to the next and every adult on the block could yell at us as if they were your parent. I watched the A-Team never realizing no one ever got shot. My Dad's Vietnam buddies and some of my grandparents WWII and Korean Veterans were the only people I knew with tattoos. The Goonies were awesome. Fame, The Cosby Show (this was before we knew about the rapes) and Family Ties, Night Court, Punky Brewster, Cheers, the Smurfs, Voltron. My sister's read Nancy Drew, I read The Hardy Boys, and had a subscription for Batman comics. Girls wore Friendship bracelets and side pony tails. The backdoor was always open, and someone was going to be yelled at for *air conditioning the neighborhood*. There was always that one field that could be used for either baseball, football, soccer or just a place to hang out. (Skyway Park in Tampa) At night we would play flashlight tag. If we didn't have the cap gun we would just get a hammer or a rock and smash the caps on the ground. My sister's had Cabbage Patch kids. I had Garbage Pail Kids Trading Cards. Sports were important. Birthday parties at McDonalds "Hey, my dad will take us if your dad will pick us up." Who else remembers Styrofoam containers and the ad campaign, "*keeps the hot side hot and the cool side cool.*"

*A blue Schwinn, Brandon, FL; A grey BMX, Myrtle Beach, SC; A black Columbia, Tampa, FL BMX; A black Marukin 12 –speed, Chesterfield, MO

ANOTHER CHILLI RECIPE

This began as one of the *one of* recipes...you know, one tomato, one can of tomatoes, one onion, one slab babay back ribs...Oh yes, did I fail to mention this is a sweet chili with ribs as the meat.

Over the years it has evolved into something not quite written down, but just known. There is still the one palm of chili powder, one palm of brown sugar, and one can of pureed black or kidney beans.

- Cook the ribs...grill, oven, whatever
- Cut ribs into three per piece (bones and all) into a large pot with at least everything mentioned above.
- Cook over the lowest heat possible for a minimum of twelve (yes, 12) hours, scraping the burnt edges back into the pot ever few hours.
- The meat will easily fall off the bone. (Leave the bones in if you want.)
- Serve over white rice.

_Remember this is a sweet, not spicy chili, so add more brown sugar to tast after ten hours of cooking.

A GIRRL I DATED

You never really realize just how little you know about a person in a new romantic relationship. Even though there is a certain amount of Christmas morning excitement as you discover and learn more every day, occasionally you hear something that will make you scream like Luke Skywalker being told he should have been sending Darth Vader father's day cards. For example; a girl I dated told me she is bi-sexual. She said she likes men because she likes attention and she desires women because she likes to have an orgasm.

DISCRIMINATION

Laws are on the books, but proving it is not easy. Okay, a person gets booted from an establishment that is open to the public. The booted out incident gets attention and a debate ensues about whether the people involved were racists. Scream and complain about civil rights all you want but understand proving *intent* in court is a lot more difficult than writing a Tweet.

Public business can refuse to serve anyone for quite frankly any non-illegal reason they want and as long as the business can come up with something even remotely reasonable sounding, law enforcement will make you leave and ask you not to come back. In some cases a person may very well be asked to leave even though they did nothing wrong. That person may be a victim of racial discrimination but you have to prove that is how it happened. If taken to court the owner or manager of the establishment could just give some kind reason, *that person was making the staff uncomfortable or another customer complained* or something which would be hard to disprove. Unless you have a recording of someone using racial slurs or the like you simply will not be able to prove discrimination.

You Are Not Welcome

TOBACCO

Tobacco is something I truly enjoy in all forms; cigars, pipes, snuff, even cigarettes. It would be terrific if there were a tobacco-supper-club in existence, I would join. No vape, no drugs, just wonderful food, exceptional company, and a seemliness never ever evening/night…sign me up! Once a month would be fine…set a menu…set the date, I'll bring some conversation and some tobacco…the Golden Leaf.

Wow, look at this, you made it all the way to the end of the book. And your disapproving authority figure insinuated you would never amount to or accomplish anything. Feel free to tear this page out and mail it to whomever that person may have been.

www.ingramcontent.com/pod-product-compliance
Lightning Source LLC
Chambersburg PA
CBHW020518290526
45786CB00002B/654